May I Kiss You on the Lips, Miss Sandra?

Also by Sandra Bernhard

Confessions of a Pretty Lady
Love, Love, and Love

May I Kiss You on the Lips, Miss Sandra?

Sandra Bernhard

Rob Weisbach Books

William Morrow and Company, Inc.   New York

Published by Rob Weisbach Books
An Imprint of William Morrow and Company, Inc.
1350 Avenue of the Americas, New York, N.Y. 10019

Library of Congress Cataloging-in-Publication Data has been
applied for.

ISBN 0-688-16471-4

Printed in the United States of America

First Edition

1 2 3 4 5 6 7 8 9 10

BOOK DESIGN BY M. KRISTEN BEARSE

www.robweisbachbooks.com

This book is dedicated to Lotus Weinstock, who once told me, "Never judge your life when you're exhausted." That quote, among so many hundreds of other gems of wisdom, has carried me through the funkiest of times. I love you, Lo. I miss you more than you could begin to imagine.

This book could never have been completed without the talent of the following people: Scott Noe, my manager, confidant, and dear friend. Mitch Kaplan, for his spontaneous madness, giant talent, and great friendship. Matthew Hunt, who just keeps coming up with some of the most genius shit I've witnessed in many moons. Dan Strone, my literary agent at the William Morris Agency, who within a week of signing me got this deal. To Rob Weisbach, who didn't hesitate to give it to me. To the huge spirit of Shelly Schultz, who brought it all together. And, of course, above all, to Herminio Sandoval for all the hours of scraping, preparing, and painting with love and happiness.

Remember what the Dalai Lama said:
"The closing of the downtown Barneys was
one of last year's greatest tragedies."

May I Kiss You on the Lips, Miss Sandra?

Hey, kids, I'm back and better than ever. You may wonder what I've been up to since the last book. Well, I've been damn busy, as you can imagine. You see, in between I fell off the fun wagon, had a lot of mind-shrinking experiences with those dark forces that lurk down every emotional alleyway—the kind of people you like to read about in *Newsweek* magazine, to quote Rick James, but do not necessarily want to have calling late into the night laying their bizarre trips on you. It was a conglomeration of these types that brought me to this tremendous personal transformation. I feel better, and I can communicate in a happier way now, so this book shouldn't bum you out—but it might piss you off or cause you to break things. Just don't forget that when you smash the phone into the wall, even *it* has consciousness. So the next time you want it to work for you, it may just say, "Hey, fuck *you*! Remember the time you were reading Sandy's book and it freaked you out, and you took it out on me? Well, now I don't feel like being so helpful to you. Tough titties." So don't hurt inanimate objects or, just like people or dogs, they just might turn and bite your ass.

I really wanted this book to come out just a few months before the apocalypse, so I could finally have a bestseller. Then I'd be able to walk amid the ruins barefoot, shards of atomic-laden glass cutting my feet, in flowing robes on the sermon mount, preaching to the deformed and hopeless that "although we managed to outlaw abortions and gay marriages, and burn black churches and convert Jews into Baptists, it just couldn't be stopped." I wanted to see Ralph Reed and Pat Buchanan resurrected above me with giant white Pratesi sheets wrapped about them, grinning goofy smiles. John Loftin is there, and Pat Robertson is too.

But don't worry, we're ass-kickin' into high gear right here with you—centered, focused like a damn Tibetan monk. We will "televise the revolution"—we will "fight the power." We're cool. Peace.

We start off by asking the old standby existential question: What is life? Right now, today, at this moment, stripped of all illusion and uncertainty. What unique cosmic convergence brought us all together tonight? Was it the first time Dr. Smith complained to Will Robinson about the pain, the pain? Was it when Jim West and Artemus Gordon, in some amazing disguise, were captured by Dr. Miguelito Loveless and his lovely companion, threatening to destroy the western world as we know it? Was it Mary Richards pouring coffee into a mug under a giant wooden letter M? With electric curlers in her hair and single-female angst brewing? Was it the day my rock station went from AM to FM as I sat in my mom's car? Was it the black light poster lit in my bedroom? Joni Mitchell on my first stereo, *Ladies of the Canyon*, Indian beaded belt on bell-bottom jeans, blue-green shag carpet, astrological wallpaper, the sexual illustrations consecrated unto me? A book about Jewish marriage? Listening in at my parents' closed door? Was it the drive from Flint to Phoenix, eating Japanese food for the first time? Shapes and forms in New Mexico—my mom coined that phrase. The ID bracelet from Jimmy who visited us with his parents who I never saw again? Was it the little boy on Concord Street, who I pulled the boots off of, spanked, and blamed over and over until Mom pulled me home? The time I wouldn't eat for a month when my parents went to

Europe? Was it when, at five years of age, I started referring to my father as good old Dad? Knowing I was pregnant after sleeping with Kevin for the first time? Touching my heart with my fist whenever Patty left? That recurring dream of rolling down a hill, out of control, next to a barbed-wire fence? Eli and the thirteenth confession? My mom's unconditional love?

Life is a series of delicate meetings held together by a spider's thread strong as a steel span, tender as the wind blowing it all away.

Herminio loves his cerveza. Herminio is my housepainter, and has been for twelve years. Now I have a classic, vintage 1930s Spanish house in the Valley. I like to keep it pristine white. I have him paint it at least once every year and a half, interior and exterior. My friends say, "Isn't that a bit obsessive, Sandra?" I say, "I live here; you don't."

When Herminio started, he was very reasonable. Fifteen hundred dollars for the entire house, inside and out. I really got to know and love him. I became close with his family. I supported him. I would even give him extra cash on the side when he needed it. He would always come over and sit in the kitchen, and we would talk for hours. He would tell me about his culture and reflect on ours. He would always say, "It makes me so sad to see such a beautiful young woman living alone in such a big house—no husband, no children. This is not good." And I would say, "You know, Herminio, you're absolutely right. My life is a fucking mess. And I'm glad you're here to remind me."

Now Herminio became quite the fixture on the gay girl circuit; everybody started using him. They loved Herminio because he was so reasonable. (You know lesbians; they love a good deal. "I'll take another corn bread basket; it's free!") Everybody used him—Melanie, Cindy, Candy, Caroline, Mimi. They drove the poor man insane. They had him doing everything, and it drove his prices through the roof.

So when he came to paint my house this year, I said, "So, Herminio, what's it going to be?" And he hemmed and hawed and hung his head sheepishly and said, "Ah, Miss Sandra, I don't like to talk about money with you; you're family—six thousand." And I said, "Herminio! I don't think so. . . . Let's make it four, and I think that's very fair!" And he says, "All right. For you, Miss Sandra, anything."

He was a little depressed this summer, and I was worried about him. So he's sitting around every day on the curb, sipping the cervezas, eating burritos out of a brown paper bag. "Herminio, work with me, honey; at least finish the interior so I can rehang my photo collection." He finally finished, and of course he did a beautiful job. On the final day, he came to collect his last check. He brought his little girl with him. I slipped her a twenty. "Here, this is for you, sweetie. Buy yourself something special. And you hide it; this is not for Daddy."

I gave Herminio his check and a cerveza, and he was in a very melancholy mood. "Ah, Miss Sandra, so many years have gone by and still you are all alone. You are such a good friend, I will never forget all that you have done for my family." He hung his head sheepishly again and hesitated. "May I kiss you on the lips, Miss Sandra?" "Herminio, have you lost your mind? Get out of my house right now! I'll see you in a year and a half."

I don't want to hang out anymore with people who are "on the move" (according to *Variety*). I can't waste my time schmoozing, kissing ass, taking lunches, listening to another writer-producer pitch me a movie and finding out there's no part in it for me. Finding this out only after I've listened with bated breath to every stinking minute. No, I'd rather have lunch in the Valley at La Salsa with my plumber, Gary, because he knows where he wants to be. He's not waiting for an opportunity to fuck anyone over. No, he gets up in the morning and feels happy to go and fix a leaky faucet, a dripping shower, a busted pipe. He has pride in himself because he's an honest man. He goes to bed at night with a clear conscience, knowing he hasn't lied once that day. When you respect yourself, you don't need to hurt anyone.

I am of the philosophy that it's always wise to be nice to working-class people because they're the ones who can make you or break you—your mechanic, electrician, gardener, plumber. For example, the morning of the big earthquake in L.A., my water heater sprang a leak. This is six in the morning and I call Gary Bergantino, my plumber, and get through. He's over in five minutes and has the damn thing fixed in fifteen. Now, as much as I like to hang with the beautiful people, I can't imagine Naomi Campbell showing up with a wrench at my house first thing in the morning.

A Possible Play

A stand-up performer doing her routine. Suddenly, she starts getting heckled. She engages the heckler.

"Where was I today? On a long transatlantic haul right back here to entertain you. I sat next to a supermodel, one name—you know her; she's a very selfish girl!"

"You're not funny."

"Well, right now, I'm not trying to be. I'm just setting up the story if you'll give me a minute, schmuck."

"Well, maybe you can move it along a little quicker, because you're boring the shit out of me!"

" 'Move it along.' 'You're not funny.' What do you want, Billy Crystal shtick? I'm not funny? Fuck you, shit for brains! I can't even see you! You don't have enough balls to show your face! Kiss my ass! I'm sharing my whole life with you. Funny is a fucking drag."

The encounter continues to the point where the performer invites the guy onstage. The play is presented at the Manhattan Theatre Club to very mediocre reviews. The comedienne is portrayed by Marisa Tomei.

Hi, I'm Sandy, and I'm an alcoholic.
I've had cheek implants, ass wings, eye lifts, skin
    dermabrasions, collagen injections in my lips, and I
    still feel so ugly.

I'm a great actress. Can't you tell?
I'm so full of shit. I feel like hell.
OK, I'll try and pull it together.
Wouldn't it be better if I just talk about the weather?

I was a stripper, a call girl, a bad waitress, an incest
    victim. My daddy called me Cherry.
I guess he should know; after all, he took it.
Can I tell you how many times he grabbed my ass and
    shook it?

I was married. I'm bi. I kissed this chick and then she
    died. I slipped and fell in so many ways. I guess I
    came to you. I keep forgetting to take it day by day.

If I had a dime for every meeting I ever missed
Or some drunken stupor and a stranger that I kissed.

Looking out from your balcony,
Will you please pour me an ice-cold martini?

I don't want to feel this way.
I guess I slipped a few steps on the ladder to AA.

Now that meeting is just for gays.
I can't take the one that's straight.

Oh, shit! Who cares if I make it anywhere.
You know for sure I'm late. Go ahead, baby, please
    don't wait.

You're a stoned cold fool for lying to yourself.

I just can't sleep at night.
I don't know how to make things right.

Did I tell you about the movie I was in?
Already told you that one, so where can I begin?

Yes, my tits are real. How much can I reveal?

I need to call someone and make amends.
I don't like the person I've become.
When will this heartache end?

I was always shy, never knew how to relate.
But when I get behind a cocktail I leave everything to fate.

I love to hear the speakers pouring out their hearts.
It can get so intense and moving.
But before I've even driven home,
I'll pour a shot and get to grooving.

What can I tell you? I'm a total mess and here I'll stay.
I guess I've slipped a rung or two on the ladder to AA.

You're a stoned cold fool and it's all over your face.
You're a stoned cold fool and you're a complete
   disgrace.

I was watching a Frank Sinatra flick the other night. It was so weird. He walked in on his ex-wife and said, "I just came here to ball you, baby!" It was 1962 and they were saying shit like that? You think about the evolution of dirty conversation and you start wondering when people first started saying "balling." Did John Kennedy say, "I want to ball you"? You'd better believe it! In Vegas, about a thousand times. "*Ich bin ein Berliner:* I'm going to ball you."

My star was defiantly on the rise—no way was I cashing in my chips. Every time I threw the dice they came up lucky sevens. I was hitting blackjack in every casino in town. I was singing my heart out in the hottest lounge in town, and nothing, I mean nothing, could have torn me away but him. The night Johnny Rosselli walked into my life I might as well have thrown everything out the window, because I did—for him I did this. But there's no one to blame but myself; like a two-bit hooker or a stripper on her way down, there I was loving him. Young, gorgeous, and still a mobster in the age of businessmen, my Johnny was hotter than a loaded gun, and here is a glimpse into the man who brought me to my knees.

He put himself on the map when he walked into the corporate headquarters of the Dunes, where I was doing a lounge act, and had a showdown with the Asians who had taken it over. He pulled out his dick and laid it on the craps table and lucky for him he hit the next four numbers that were rolled. He had those Asian bastards screaming, "You bring evil spirits to Dunes," and maybe they were right, because a couple of years later the place was gone. Once the screaming was settled, Johnny put his dick back in his sharkskin suit and they made him the general manager.

He made me fall in love with him with the same force. He wanted me to give it all up and have his babies. And when I did, he started screwing the star of the Moulin Rouge.

You wake me in the morning with such bad news.

I got nothing to lose.
You interrupt my sleep, you disturb my dreams,
You leave me with no way to choose.

When you walked out on me this morning,
You shook me to my core.
You know all I did was cry,
And if that wasn't enough, I'll tell you more.
You left me here to die.
When you woke me up this morning,
You left me with nothing but the blues.

I cursed the day I met you,
You brought me nothing but pain.
You see, I curse the day I met you,
You brought in all the rain.
You made me question my religion,
You brought me down to shame.
My heart's an open book now.
Go ahead, read between the lines.
My heart's an open book now
Without poetry or rhyme.
It's such a sad, sad story—is it really mine?

This morning you interrupted my sleep,
You woke me with such bad news.
You disturbed my dreams this morning,
And you left me with the blues!

Oh, yeah, we had a lot of fun. I never laughed so damn hard. Sitting in a big burgundy velvet suite at the Sands with the whole gang. Frank, Shirley (before she went cuckoo), Sammy (who used to grab me and force me to do that cheesy dance routine I'd been doing down on the Strip), when they all met me. As a matter of fact, that's how I met Jack. They had all piled into the Horseshoe for the midnight show. I had worked up this routine that involved all the different styles of Latin dancing and music. Cha-cha, rumba, salsa, and then, for the finale, I shook my big ass and rubbed my tits on a Castro look-alike, whose cigar exploded simultaneously with me dropping my top. A lot of smoke and sparks that brought the house down night after night. Well, when the pack got wind of it, and with Jack popping into town, they knew it was a must-see! All that junk going on with Cuba. I was so nervous when the girls all came back to tell me Mr. President was coming to check me out.

I took extra care with my eyelashes and wig. I trimmed and plucked. Well, I was a nervous wreck, because I knew in some deep place that I was going to have my moment with him. By the time the show was over, he would be hooked. I could seem real nonchalant and breezy, which would turn him on like crazy. I felt him, you know, in my dreams when I was just wandering around. I had this sense of him, the way he smelled, his cologne and big cigars, his salty skin, that smile, those gorgeous white teeth, the bulge in his shorts. I watched and he knew it. Of course, I was falling in love, a very stupid thing for a girl in Vegas. You see, I was young and confident, and no one was telling us not to imagine having it all in 1961. There weren't any women's libbers yakking up all that horse crap. We had our own morals and politics.

I know a lot of the girls Jack made it with, and I can tell you not one of them wasn't in love and didn't care about this country. It was our patriotic duty to give the president some pleasure. We never asked twice what we would do for our country. He was working so hard you wanted to give him some escape. Oh, sure, we all knew he wasn't going to leave Jackie. We weren't stupid! She was his princess, and I guess we were ladies-in-waiting. And oh, baby, did we wait, late into the night, primped and powdered, exhausted but all pumped up.

I'll never forget that first night Jack came to see me. It was probably a couple of months after he saw my revue, and he *loved* it! He started calling. We would talk quietly, and he loved my voice, as you can imagine. Just like Jackie and Marilyn put together, breathy and longing.

I was pacing around like some caged cat. Hot and sweaty, beads of salt water rolling down in between my tits. Pouring cold martinis, arranging tchotchkes all over the apartment, straightening paintings left, right, and center. I was nuts! The advance men came by at eleven. Strictly professional, checking around, buttoned-up, no-nonsense. They asked a few questions, which I respected and understood. They smiled knowingly. Did I care? Of course not! They knew, but I had class, and don't think that doesn't go a long way.

Jack loved a good conversation. He didn't dig bimbos or drunks. He wanted a hot dame, clean and up. I was a natural, never had to force the personality. Oh, baby, when he knocked on my door and I opened it up, well, what can I say, I was dripping wet. I looked him right in the eye, took his hand, and made him feel right at home. He *loved* it!

Of course, you would think it all happened real quick. A splash of scotch, dick in hand, a BJ, and a piss in the can—over and out. But erase that negative thinking, boys and girls. *Au contraire,* he was shy, like a teenage boy, can you believe it? Well, you're going to have to, because that's simply the way it was. Don't forget, we had talked a lot on the phone, so we got to know each other slowly.

I got under his skin and he set mine on fire. Maybe I was pushing it. If anybody, it was me. I drank vodkas straight up. I sat on the chair across from him. I mean, can you imagine? There he was, the leader of the western world, sitting in my joint. He told me right away how classy it was, how interesting my choice in art. He was riveted to my glass menagerie. We talked about Tennessee Williams; he knew him. This was killing me, because I knew I was falling in love, big time. It was like anticipating the pain of losing him before it all began. He must have picked up on it because he got up and stood behind me and started rubbing my shoulders. It was the first instant he touched me. I had to hold back the tears. I threw on the brakes before I scared him. I knew it, and I had to switch gears like that. The last thing he needed was some broad getting all weepy on him. What a big turnoff.

I caressed his hands as they rested on my shoulders. The energy coming from behind me was explosive, and then I couldn't stand it another minute, so I pulled him over me and slid down to the carpet. "Jesus, Jack, I can't take it, honey. You're so fucking hot, I just want to give it to you like you've never had it before!" I undid his belt and unzipped those pants so fast he didn't know what hit him. Ella was swinging out of the speakers. Everything went hazy when he popped out of his shorts—angels blew trumpets, lilacs bloomed, a hurricane ripped through my head. Girls, I gave it to him slowly, torturing, teasing. I was all lips and tongue. I could feel him looking down at me, smiling, the lights bouncing off his teeth. "Ooooohh, baby" and "Christ almighty, let's run away to Acapulco. I'll give you anything you want, stay right there"—he said it all. I stayed tuned right in. I managed to wiggle out of my dress and get my tits up to his face. Wait a minute—how did I manage that one? Don't ask.

We crawled into the bedroom. "Oh, Chickie Baby, I love you!" I blurted it out. He didn't seem to mind; Frank called him that and he had it monogrammed on his robe. Chickie Baby! He didn't seem to mind. Kids, I rode him like a bucking bronco. We screamed and sweated and lit the town up like a thousand neon signs. Lights dimmed on the Strip in honor of the moment. I bit him so hard I thought I drew blood. He slapped my ass and I laughed, I cried. We rested and whispered all these crazy secrets.

I saw a wisp of morning light trying to sneak its ugly ass into my bedroom, and I got sad for a minute; I knew he'd have to leave soon. I couldn't fool myself into thinking he was going to sleep the day away in my arms, but I got the surprise of my life when he asked me to make him steak and eggs for breakfast. I tied a robe around me and he lit up a cigar and lay back on my satin sheets, puffing away. Chirping out to me in the kitchen, like a morning bird, asking a million questions about where I was from, my family. . . . He devoured everything, including me. Lo and behold, we did fall into the most divine sleep.

The phone rang at ten. It was Bobby, looking for his brother. It sounded intense, so I left the room and heard him talking in hushed tones, laughing a little. He mentioned my name. I hugged myself. I was cleaning the dishes when he came out dressed, all tousled and gorgeous. "Baby, I've got to go. I got this crazy job to do, you know, talking to the Russians, passing a few laws. Whatever, last night was sensational. I think we've got to do it again, soon. Real soon." He took me in his arms and I inhaled every ounce of him into my lungs. We walked to the door and he kissed me good-bye. I couldn't speak. I know I would have regretted every word. I'm sure it was for the best.

I never saw Jack again. Things were crazy. What with test ban treaties and the Bay of Pigs, he wasn't making it out to Vegas so much. I didn't take it personally, believe me. The rumors didn't bother me either, even if he was seeing Marilyn. Who could blame her? The love he gave me in that one night has carried me through all these years. I turn the television off whenever they speak about him— those same clips over and over—because the movie I've got inside my head is the only picture I need. As if it happened yesterday—which, as far as I'm concerned, it did.

I stayed with the show until Valerie Perrine took over in 1967.

She'll have engraved in marble ten reasons not to have sex.

An older blond big-tittied woman is spreading her ass and sticking her head through, singing a tune lamenting gay men. Superimposed behind her is a big photo of a naked man. "You can't get any dick today, because all the good guys are gay. Oh, hell, it doesn't matter anyway because I'm just a big, huge, gaping hole so there ain't no pole big enough for me and my twat. Hey, looky here, I'm no queer, but you sure are, my dear." She looks back at the photo and sticks out her tongue.

Some people leave such an indelible mark on your life that there is almost no experience that you can't relate back to them. Brenda Vaccaro is one of those touchstones in my life. For instance, that dress you bought in the medina in Marrakech—well, Brenda has one exactly like it. Of course, it has more red in it than yours, but it's the very same idea. Now this chicken dish is divine; it reminds me of the time Brenda threw a fabulous dinner party and prepared her famous stuffed breast of chicken, so reminiscent of your recipe. You raise rare orchids? Oh, this is mad. Why, Brenda just has a green thumb that never quits. She travels with her plants and manages quite nicely to keep them all going strong, along with her career. She is such an inspiration to everyone! "I love this song, though Brenda's not really a fan of pop music." "Do you want to catch a movie tonight? There's that new Barbra Streisand festival playing at Film Forum. Didn't you love Brenda Vaccaro in *The Mirror Has Two Faces*? I thought she was amazing!" "You know, Brenda would never make me go with her to a gallery opening the way you are right now."

The stage is set in 1960s modern: a shag rug, globe lamps, Mies van der Rohe, Saarinen tulip end tables, Jackson Pollock drip paintings. "Cast Your Fate to the Wind" is playing loudly, obscuring the telephone conversation of the woman onstage who paces up and down, crying, her face alternating between spasms of pain and forced mocking laughter. She lights up a cigarette, throws the match down into one of those blue ashtrays, solid crystal. She is talking on a Princess phone, so the wire drags along behind her. She pours a drink from a simple decanter, tosses in some ice cubes, and belts back her poison. Finally, she sits down in an easy chair. The music fades, and we can begin to hear bits of her conversation. "Well, let me put it this way: if he ever wants to see me again, the first-class plane ticket had better be accompanied by a giant Harry Winston stone. . . . I don't give a damn about his wife. I've heard the story at least a thousand times. . . . Well, I'm ready to walk in and snap her out of the coma and tell her the whole sordid story—oh, that'll wake her ass up. Maybe they can trade places. I'm sure she's a very nice person. She probably fell asleep in the middle of one of his long-drawn-out, self-involved tales of woe and figured it would just be easier to stay asleep. A lot less work; she's been able to maintain her figure and keep her friends. With a jerk like that driving you nuts, she might have chosen the perfect option!

The thing we've missed most about Sandra's one-woman show is the dancing. Those lavish dance numbers just blew us away!

All over town there are big, fabulous billboards for hepatitis! Big purple billboards with yellow eyes. Who knew a virus could be so much fun? "Fairy tales can come true, it can happen to you . . . if you're young at heart."

Good evening. I'm in a slightly sophisticated feeling. With a chance of a sexy meeting. Did you want to move closer? I suggest that you do. Want to whisper in my ear? I can make all your tension disappear.

Good evening. I decided to put myself out on a limb and wear a dress that is very revealing. Hello there! I know you've heard it a thousand times before, but let it go—it could be the original one of a kind. Wind it up and watch it spin; come on in. The city twinkles below, like a thousand million stars that bubble and glow. The stage is set. Come and get it; I've chilled down the bubbly to a crackling frosty 15 degrees. The stage is set; it's up to you and me to fall. I just want you to know—I want to make this an affair and I'm willing to share it. I've chilled down the bubbly to a crackling 22; I've hors d'oeuvres—they are delicious—just for you. I'll rub your neck; I'll massage your thighs. The shit I'll do to you will make you want to cry.

Good evening. I've been in the kitchen all day preparing a little something to sway your emotions, drown you in an ocean, and if you have a notion for love, you're the man of my dreams and I want you to know how I feel. When we lie down on my bed and the sheets are so cozy, all the neighbors will gather around and listen through the walls. It's something to be heard; I can't blame them for being nosy.

Good evening. I think this is the beginning of rebeliev-ing, about the games, the parties, the partying, the drugs, the such. I will not be deceiving; I'm going to hold you so close and tight, you'll see just how I treat you right, my big tall handsome man. I know you've had some games played on your head, but that's all in the past. Let me undress you; maybe I'm too bad but let me caress you, I love you. Maybe it's too soon to say I love you, you're in my life for good, knock on wood. I don't want to let you go, no no no no! Let's go all the way, hey hey hey!

You're such a gentleman. I love your suits, the part in your hair. I don't really care what anybody thinks or what anybody feels. It's all about you tonight, you're the man, and I want to take you down, going to love you now, so good evening. Love you, baby, drive me crazy, got to go.

When anger and hatred turn into passion and sex.
When loneliness and love turn into boredom and fear.

Recently I was fortunate enough to take in an exciting cabaret moment at a hip downtown club called Shit. Friends and I piled into an exclusive stage-side booth to take in the full impact of the extravaganza. Without a doubt, the high-light of the show was the young, buxom, fire-eating bru-nette. The house lights lowered, signaling her entrance. As the gauzy curtains parted and the smoke machines made their magic, I saw the talented girl appear from stage left. I'm sure she was a striking beauty, although I couldn't catch a sharp view of her, owing to the moody lighting. Through the flashing strobes and blinding minikliegs, my fire-eater swallowed torch after torch, wowing even the most cynical audience member. As a finale, she blew a fireball that nearly set the house ablaze. The crowd lost its collective mind.

After her performance, I summoned up enough courage to approach her at the bar.

"Excuse me, but I think you might like me to buy you an icy-cold water!"

As she turned around to answer, I noticed that my lovely fire-eater was covered from head to toe in blisters and skin grafts. I fled in horror—not because I couldn't appreciate the inner beauty beneath her disfiguring scars, but because the sight of her brought back all of the pain and trauma of a burn I once suffered myself.

I had been shopping in a popular, mildly upscale national

store when a sheer paisley blouse caught my eye. As you may know, I am a fan of paisley, not to mention the sheer aspect, which was right up my alley. I bought the blouse without hesitation and wore it to a disco that very night. Music was blaring and I was feeling the groove, surrounded by a bevy of hot muscle boys dancing to Janet Jackson. Without warning, I was engulfed in flames. If it weren't for my sexy dance partners, who wrapped me in a Persian rug, I would've looked like that fire-eater.

The next day I rushed back to the store to replace my paisley blouse. When I didn't find it on the rack, I went to the cash register to inquire. Mounted on the counter was a sign announcing the recall of the SHEER PAISLEY BLOUSE because it didn't meet the flame-retardant codes! Admittedly, my body temperature was slightly elevated, but that fucking blouse just spontaneously combusted! I'm scarred for life, not to mention my new phobia of patterns and printed fabric.

A Taste of Honey

Everything is as it was and will be again. There were many times, walking around Lake Washington, that Kurt would take off his sweater and wrap it around me, the cold blowing. The dark sky's painting shadows on his lovely face. Quietly we spoke, pieces of leaf in his hair—here, there, and everywhere. I don't cry now. I'm one of the few who have managed to remain strong, trusting that we will be together again in the many seasons of our lives and times. Kurt was a gentle soul and don't you know he brought out the rose in me and our generation. There's always a voice that speaks to us in the darkest of times, and yes, I could have saved him, but somehow in death his power has multiplied. So I must honor that beautiful truth he inspired in all of us. But I might say the touch of his hand on mine will haunt me forever. The spirit he called "teen" left a light on in my heart, in the craziest of moments rushing by. I won't lie—I love you, Kurt. So this song was written on the wind, for you walk among us still. . . .

I can remember when you were so cool and cutting-edge, when you saved me from jumping off a ten-story ledge.

Now you don't seem to care. You just lie around all day. I can't even look at you. I don't like the music you play. You're so stuck in your way.

Nothing interests you. You've got nothing to say. I always looked up to you like some guru or sage, but now you just look old for your age.
Sorry, but you look old for your age.

I guess in time everything disintegrates. You have no passion in the areas of love and hate. I'm sick of sitting around here when you wake up so late.
You gave it up too soon, left it all to fate.

Everything you think, it's just redundancy. It's driving me up a wall, your new philosophy. I used to love you as a guru or a sage, but, sorry, you just look old for your age.

When did you lose all your enthusiasm and joy? How did you turn into a bitter old man from a sweet little boy? Why did it become such a drag to play with a toy? I know you don't want to hear all this white noise.

.

I can remember when I depended on you completely, when you could explain things so patiently and discreetly, the way you lie beside me with words that were so sweetly. When did you trade your spirit in and beat me? Christ, I looked up to you like a guru or a sage, but you're tired and you look old for your age.

All those times you saved me by salvation, dragged me by the hair out of fucked-up situations. You could have been Moses, conferring about creation, but instead you put your feelings on probation.

So, if this is how it's going to be, then perhaps I should set you free. There is nothing more; it's all a blank page and I am tired of your tirades and your pretentious charades, and I always believed you were a guru or a sage; but, baby, it is a fact—you just look old for your age.

This is a story I hope no one has told you yet. I've been close to it for a long time, so if you don't like it, I can't say for sure how it'll make me feel. When I first met Lisa, I was a young boy, open raw like a dog-licked wound, kind of scabby and oozing because that's how I felt—unsure, teetering on life's rickety ladder. Maybe you would have liked me better then, but that's not my story or the thing I'm concerned about right now. You see, I was in love with this girl from Texas. She was a topless dancer here in New York—amazing, real American beauty, all whipped-up blond hair, frothy, foamy, salty like a delicious margarita. She smelled like a blossom that rode in on a truck across this big country, smoking in cafés along the highway in the middle of the night, waiting, breakfasts all day long, dropping coins in the pay phone to talk to the little boy she'd left behind. That killed me, you know, because she loved that kid for sure. When she hit New York and got herself a job at Goldfingers, she wanted desperately to make a life for herself, sticking tips in her shoe, doing thing with other girls for money, the stuff men talk about and the rich ones live for. She was in danger most of the time, calling collect to her husband, who listened, hung up, and went back to his life as quickly as possible. I entered the picture on Fifty-fourth Street in the fall. It was just at the moment that I wanted to leave, wishing that this were another time and place so I could find a country that had yet to be discovered, some romantic ocean liner to take me to Istanbul or Persia, not like now with the earth savaged, people-controlled, fucked over. Shipments of plutonium from Georgia to Tennessee—no, better to stay in New York and let it all come to me, because the best of the world was here anyway. I was walking past Studio 54 around back and she just came up to me, exclaiming, "I've never met anybody like you before; you're so beautiful you could be a boy or a girl. Would you mind if I hug you?" Of course, I let her because it was a cold night; I was out walking and lonely too.

Dad cuts lines for Christmas.

On a recent flight over California, a father was observed sharing a Christmas moment with his son. "Let me go blow my nose real quick and I'll come back and divvy it up. I hope you like what I got you this year, son; it's good shit."

I can hear the blood pulsing through my veins and arteries. It's pounding inside my head like a native drum beating out a warning in the African wild. Lights are flashing furiously, but I can't focus because I don't want to. I can't—I'm terrified, I'm thirsty, I stink, and I've peed in my pants. Well, we've all seen those movies about space travel and what happens when the gyroscope whirls out of control. The tumbling starts and your forehead turns beet-red, like a tomato ready to collapse or explode. I saw an actual document of this in training, where they sent up a rhesus monkey in the late 1950s. There it was, with its little fingers and freaked-out face, strapped in tight; then something went haywire and the monkey started screaming, then it swelled up and splattered all over the capsule. I cried my eyes out when they showed it to me. I had to run to the bathroom and barf, but it was good to see it and accept that many things can happen when you make a commitment to the unknown, as it was right now to me.

I'm thinking about the monkey, my family, the faces of fifty people who put me here. Voices are fading in and out, but it doesn't matter; I'm ready for anything. All the people there are depending on me, you see, because what I've just left behind is on the verge of extinction. Earth, as I have known it my whole life, is over. I am one of many people chosen to save the human race. A series of earthquakes, fires, floods, and other disasters have been brought on by environmental abuses too complex to unravel. Big business, controlling the government, has finally succeeded in pushing human survival over the edge. There's almost no one left to trust. Panic has overwhelmed the sanest of us. This mission, which was meticulously placed by the Alternative Life Projection (ALP), had to be suddenly escalated when the Volga River caught fire and burned up. They called me Saturday morning at four-thirty. My German shepherd started crying. The letters I had prepared for my parents and friends were hastily dumped into the mailbox. There wasn't time to call anyone or pack a bag. I grabbed my prayer book and Star of David. We flew out to a remote desert rendezvous launch strip near the Great Salt Lake. I was briefed and debriefed, there was a minister to offer prayers. I picked up a handful of dirt and held it to my nose; there wasn't time for anything else, emotions were confused—and it was then I remembered how long it had been since I'd been really loved by someone. The team set me carefully into the spacecraft, my home, injected me with tranquilizers so that I would sleep until I was so deep into space I couldn't come back. I saw the Earth fade below me very fast; I began to dream, Wernher von Braun in a black-and-white film from the 1950s, so sure of the future. I dreamed of my mother's warm kisses, the bubbles in Canada Dry ginger ale, smells of buses merging into traffic, fists of politicians clenched in mock anger. I felt the pressure pounding in my chest, unable to wake. But then something surges through the electrodes connected to my head and I am jarred wide awake, wondering what makes me the kind of woman never willing to cling to false hopes. Here I am searching for the survival of a heartless race, knowing that no one will be coming to save me, and wasn't that going to be a fact that might not drive me insane?

Forget Gen X. Now there's the Y Generation.

"Why do I have to pay my own phone bills? Why do I have to call you and tell you how sad I am for you because your best friend of twenty-two years died? Why, why, *why*?"

The little waifish girls singing about "such simple things, life is sad and so tender, she always has a boyfriend by one side, and a girl who's ambiguous on the other. I don't know. I think I'm more straight than gay. I'm scared, will you please accept me this way?"

No.

It's about love.
It's about forgiveness.
It's about letting go.

I'm not saying yes.
I'm not saying no.
I can't tell you to stay
Or, with all my heart, please go.
Our love has been a mystery
In spite of its short history.
With all of our confusion
I know it's not illusion.
When you're lying in my arms
And we dream before we sleep,
I'm transfixed by your sweet charms.
Maybe I've fallen in too deep.
Will someone please wake me?
Take me back to where I was before.
If you must go on and take me
To where there remains an open door.
I know you still want me to love you.
Can I just leave you standing here?
To the edge of a cliff I will go.
Is there a way to relieve your fear?
I try to stay away—
Your tender face does haunt me.

I promise to be brave.
Will my heart please not taunt me?
Wherever you may wander
In this pinprick of a world,
Never bleed your soul to waste
For you'll always be my girl.

The most romantic thing anyone's said to me in recent months: "I want to do heroin with you sometime." That is so sweet!

The one time I thought I'd get a little frisky, I was in Amsterdam with my then girlfriend Sally. She was a hairdresser. Now, Sally was a trip. Sally grew up in the Valley, and she was the original Valley girl. We once drove past North Hollywood High and I said, "Hey, Sally. Didn't you graduate from there?" She said: "No, I shined it on and went to Hawaii." So Sally and I are hanging out in Amsterdam, and I said: "You know what? I feel like getting stoned. Let's go have a hash cookie . . . cool . . . why not? It's Amsterdam—live it up!" So I went and ate half the hash cookie. It tastes like an oatmeal cookie, no big deal. And we wandered around the red-light district. We went to a sex show. Sally was smoking pot, blowing it in my face, and halfway through it I said: "You know what? I'm a little hungry. Let's go get a nosh. I'm going to have another half a hash cookie." So we went back to the Bulldog. I inhaled the thing! And then I got a little buzz going, a little buzz. We went dancing at the Milky Way. I said: "Let's go back to the hotel." We're driving in a taxi; suddenly everything became funny, right? We drove past Anne Frank's house— "Anne Frank's house, that is a fucking scream!" We get back to our faux-American hotel, because the Dutch love anything kind of American, right? It's a hotel in the round with rust-colored carpet, so it took a while to find the room. We get back. I'm ordering up cheese sandwiches and snacks. I said: "I'm taking a bath, Sall." I get in the bath, I have a picture of me in that bath, and it was not a pretty moment for Sandy. And just as I stepped out, the shit really hit me full-tilt boogie. I mean, I am hallucinating, I'm freaked out. "Sally, I think you better get me to a hospital. I am so sick." I said, "And there's my passport and some cash on the counter." (Even when I'm fucked up I'm in total control.) So I get dressed, we go downstairs, we go up to the concierge, and Sall says: "My friend is really sick. Can you get an ambulance?" The concierge snickers. "Did she eat a hash cookie?"

I'm sitting on the curb, with my head in my hands. And I'm thinking, "Oh, my G-d. What am I going to tell my parents? How will they ever understand when my body is shipped home? I can't believe that I've done this. I'm twenty-nine and I'm in my Saturn return. Why did I ever get fucked up? I love you, Mommy. I love you, Daddy."

So we finally get a taxi, and he's going 20 miles per hour, but I swear he's going 150. And we get to the hospital. I cling to the doctor: "Doctor, am I ever going to think normal thoughts again? Will I ever remember things, or who I am?" She gave me a shot of Librium. I threw up in the sink. Then Sally held me, for the first time ever, on a hard wooden bench.

So, to all you romantics out there, the next time you think that I'm going to mainline some H with you, please think again.

So you're waiting for your ship to come in.
I'm over here waiting on the other side.
Did our love ever really begin? I hope it never ends
Or I'll break down and cry.
You say you're confused, but you're a strong girl.
Don't be afraid of the judgment of the whole damn
    world.
Can't your love guide you to just be sure?
This time . . . this time, girl, your eyes betray some of
    the things you say.
I know how you really feel; just let your heart reveal.
I loved you right from the start.

I never was afraid
That you would break my heart.
I want to take away your doubt and pain.
Please let go of that useless shame.
I'll be waiting for you all the same.

No blame for you, my girl,
If I had to let you go.
Just so you really know.

Then I'll take the fall this time
Because I love you.

Why do we stop a love that is so true?
You have so many things pulling you away.
Can't you just give it up, come and be with me?
Set your mind at ease.
You'll never find someone to make you good,
To show you the right way to be as you should.
I only want the best
For with all my heart
My girl.

When blondes fall, they fall so hard.

You know, I always admired Courtney Love. I always thought of Courtney as a blur, a tear, a bruise. So tender, so fragile, you know? I was performing up in Seattle a couple of years ago, and I thought: This is my perfect opportunity to hook up with her. I just really wanted her to come to my show, so I got in touch with her assistant, and he said, "Yeah, she's flying back from L.A. tonight, and I think she can make it."

"That will be cool."

And then he surprised me and popped by with the nanny and Frances Bean to my sound check. Frances was in a little bit of a cranky mood—"This is too loud for me!" I said, "For Christ's sake, your father was Kurt Cobain, your mother's Courtney Love! I'm too loud? Get the kid out of here! I don't need this shit!"

So I'm onstage and I am so tapped into my source, I'm channeling down things I have never said before. And I swear, I felt Courtney reach out to me three or four times, we were so connected. And I rushed offstage and said to my manager, "I'm not even going to change—just bring her back; I can't wait to meet her." And he said, "Honey, she missed her flight; she wasn't here."

I was heartbroken. I was devastated. We flew down to Portland the next day, and I was getting ready that afternoon about half an hour before the show, and the phone rang—"Hey, man, it's me, it's Courtney. What's happening?"

"It's so great to hear from you." And she started rambling on about everything. Talking about feminism, Naomi Wolf versus Camille Paglia, and fashion, and then she described the first time we had met, when I stepped over her in a snowbank on the Lower East Side. She just jumped from one topic to the next, stream of consciousness. I finally just got into the shower with the phone. I was shaving, shampooing, douching, sweating. I finally said, "Courtney, I'd love to keep talking but I've got to get to the theater." She said, "OK, be back in your room by eleven-fifteen"— already controlling me.

I ran to the club and did the fastest, tightest twenty-four-minute set I've ever done. And I rushed back to my hotel room with about half an hour to spare, so I could get back in that mood—you know, feeling good, relaxed. And I lay down in my bed and I put the phone right next to the pillow—because you know those hotel phones, they are a fuck-over moment, "brrring-ding-ding," you can barely hear them—just in case I fell asleep. So, 11:20 rolls around and no Courtney; 12:45, 2:15, 3:59, 6:92. I finally popped a couple of melatonin and talked myself down: "Don't worry, Courtney loves you. She just got sidetracked."

OK. A few months later I am in New York, and she's going to be performing at Roseland. So I get some tickets and put together a really cute outfit—miniskirts are back in. So I put on a wool mini, agnès b. sweater, some tights, and flat boots—you know, youthful, fresh, fun. So I go to the show, and I'm standing by the stage and she walks off and does a dramatic double take, and she grabs me by the hand and pulls me into the dressing room, and Frances Bean is on the floor playing with her dolls. Courtney gets on the cellular phone and starts trying to track down Trent Reznor of Nine Inch Nails, who's down in New Orleans staying under the pseudonym "Mr. Shit." This goes on for forty-five min-utesand I am thinking to myself, "This is so funky . . . so rock 'n' roll . . . so cutting-edge." Then we leave and we go to an AIDS benefit party in her honor, and we're posing with the paparazzi, and she tries to kiss me on the mouth—"Please, Courtney, not here. Maybe later in your hotel suite." So we hang for a while, and it's a scene, and then we leave. We were going to say good night to each other, and there are some fans there and they say, "Hi, Sandra, it's really nice to meet you," and she says, "Get the fuck out of her face, man, she doesn't need this shit!" And I'm like, "Wow, I feel like Wynona Ryder." A woman stronger than me?

I get up early the next morning, and I write, compose, and rewrite the most incredible fax to Courtney, just telling her how much she has affected me:

Dearest Courtney:
You have changed my life forever. You are such an artist and you have totally inspired me. Thank you so much for spending time with me last night and sharing your heart. Please stay in touch with me and be a part of my life forever. I think you are amazing.

Love,
Sandra

Well, a year and a half goes by; she's gone full Hollywood. She's hanging out with Amanda De Cadenet; they're wearing fabulous, funky vintage dresses and matching tiaras; going to the Oscars; she's doing subtle changes, just little things . . .

One day I'm driving home on a Saturday up La Brea after shabbat, because I never miss a Torah reading, and I am on my way to see one of my oldest, dearest friends, who is not well. Suddenly I look over at somebody staring at me, and she vaguely resembles Courtney, and I roll down the window and she's, like, "Hey, it's me—Courtney! Let's go to Red and get a caffe latte!" So I say, "I'll see my friend later," and we end up at Insomnia and she pulls out a twenty and buys me an ice-blended, and that really touches me. And we sit and she talks for a while about spirituality and movie offers. I sit riveted to her. She just looks so perfect and beautiful. And suddenly I really feel overwhelmed, and I run out to the curb and throw up.

And I start thinking to myself: "You know, Courtney, you may live to be a hundred and never have a wrinkle. But what plastic surgeon is going to fix the scars in your heart, baby? Who's going to go in there and sew up the wounds in your heart?"

Looking at Stevie Nicks is like looking at myself, and when I feel I've been thinking too much about myself, then it's hard to see my reflection or hers.

She has been an angel visiting hell, escaping by the fine thread of a spider's web, the finest and yet strongest fiber in nature's realm. She is pulled up from her own despair by the spider weaving there. She could have succumbed to the madness, but instead she gave it all to the lovers and robbers of the heart, saved by nature.

I miss Courtney Love and I love Joni Mitchell. Where is Laura Nyro, do you know?

Does Patti Smith think about me anymore, or would she prefer that I just blow?

Doesn't mean a damn thing without a friend, like Carole King.

Marianne Faithfull stays loyal to her muses. Why did Janis leave? Was it only to confuse us?

Aretha won't fly so she takes the midnight train. Tammy left so long ago that Marvin overflowed with pain. Cher can only flip her hair; we can't find her anywhere.

Singing with the angels, shattered glasses from the start, Karen C has lost her heart.

Nina Simone is waiting indignantly for her share of *Porgy* money.

Miss Ross is flashing an ivory smile. Does it define those Motown blues?

Tina's legs are legends she won't let Ike abuse.

Dolly keeps her distance in danger keeps the stranger.

Chaka went right through the fire and took us to the limit.

Stevie Nicks will twirl in lace in platform boots she can embrace.

Dionne can see into the future. It's done nothing for her past.

Nico was a superstar in the perfect role she was cast.

Abbey Lincoln is on the edge. Where, oh, where is Sister Sledge?

Sheila E., Lisa, and Wendy ran from the Purple Paisley little boy, who dangled them all like a broken toy.

Miss Gladys Knight left her Pips; it's resting now on Missy Elliott's hips.

Lil' Kim, with bleached-blond extensions, came to shake up all pretensions.

Ginger chose the road less traveled and watched the Spice Girls come unraveled.

If it only lasts for a little while, let all the women of rock 'n' roll find a way to express their style.

And let Miss Jett grow back her shag, light a fag, and take a drag.

Give me Ann and Nancy kicking it out, and never let their candle fade or completely blow out.

I had to learn to chill out with my friends.

"You know, it is kind of weird. I worked out with Steven this morning and then we went to Eighteenth and Eighth for lunch. He walked me home and we left it that we were going to have dinner tonight. And I was getting ready and then he called me at 6:30 P.M. and told me that this guy had called him for a date and did I mind if we didn't have dinner. Well, I was really hurt because we had made these plans and he knows how vulnerable I am right now and at the last minute he cancels. Well, how am I supposed to feel? Now what am I going to do? It is too late to make dinner plans. I guess I will just go to the Bus Stop and have a Greek salad by myself."

If they didn't want to spend twenty-four hours a day with me, I was hurt, constantly questioning what had gone wrong in the friendship. I think I drove them completely nuts.

You don't own anyone. When I realized that I needed my space, I started giving it to my friends.

Lotus Weinstock was a legend. I had already heard about the brilliant bit she did in the Miss America Pageant before I met her at Ye Little Club in Beverly Hills the first night I ever went up to perform. Lo thought I was adorable in khaki culottes and safari jacket with laced-up espadrilles and a straw hat. She took me under her wing and became my mentor, spiritually and comedically. She and her daughter, Lil, were family; we celebrated the Jewish holidays together. We performed together in the Belly Room at the Comedy Store, staging a mock fight at the end of every performance. We had this ritual of talking to each other under our breath, simultaneously answering and asking mock questions. She was the sister I never had.

Tonight is my dear Lotus's birthday. What an inspiration she is to me, what a blessing and a mitzvah to know her, to be able to touch her and give her love and therefore receive so much in return. The look in her eyes; her tears; her smile as bright as ever, encompassing all the light of the world, illuminating all of us with such joy and blessing. We all sang so she could sing, sitting like a queen and a baby on her couch with so many beautiful things from her mommy, with Lily standing by her as she has since I've known them. Lily, five, clutching a tiny little violin, and now such a woman taking such care of her mommy. I have learned so much from Lo, when her words flowed effortlessly. And yet now, when they come in bits and pieces, I learn things from the depths of her soul that have brought me such passion and understanding that I stand humbled by the presence of the light and G-d, with all his splendor and true beauty, channeled through my sweet, sweet friend, Lo. Sing it, sing it, sing it, sing it high, sing it Lo.

Happy happy birthday, my love, from all of us who adore you!!!

I don't know how to be with you
and I don't know how to be without you.

You are so beautiful
across a table with sparkly things in your hair.

I want to be able not to want you so badly,
to just observe you, like standing in a museum staring
    for hours—

Longing to touch the texture of paint
or the coolness of a statue,

But knowing I cannot.
At night with the light of the street shining on your
    face.

You sleep, so I stay quiet and breathe gently.
Who are we when our lives intersect like this?

I think I know your thoughts because we feel so much
    the same.
I long for you to wake up and talk to me.
I miss you here, twelve inches away,

More than I could possibly miss you on the other side
   of the world.
So I travel with you in my dreams
   to places we may never go in waking hours.

We can never own any of this.
I can't demand your time or your dedication.

For sure I love you the most when I'm able to let it
   fly—
your soul, that is, which is where I love you the most.

A Scene from an Independent Film

Opening shot: two women driving in a convertible Saab on their way to Palm Springs. Sergio Mendes and Brasil 66 is blasting. The woman driving is very into it, singing along. She is happy, looks to be in her early thirties but is in fact older. The girl next to her looks to be sixteen but is in fact older. She is not digging the music and turns it off. Leslie, the older woman, is hurt and kind of shocked in that awful weird way that happens when someone likes someone and has to play it cool, especially when the younger girl—Mia— is so sexy and superdangerous.

You would almost expect her to pull out a syringe and plunge it into her arm. It's obvious Leslie has lost control, and only her years of experience as a hard ass are keeping her grounded.

"Do you mind if I turn it off?"

Leslie (with hesitation covering anger): "Sure, that's fine. I mean, it's Sergio Mendes. You've got to get into it. Listen to this; it doesn't get any better. For Christ's sake, this is pure romance, love, raw sex, it's totally fucking hot, but you go ahead, turn it off. Let me just finish this line: "The sky is filled with stars, so many stars, which one is mine?" OK, go ahead and turn it off. What turns you on, Mia? Heavy D, *Waterbed Hev* or something? Because, of course, we have that in the selection as well. Being in the 'hood with all your sisters, checking out the fine m-f-ers, because you love doing it doggy style and telling all your actress friends about it at the Sky Bar? Do you tell them about us? I doubt it, because this is so shameful and wrong. Real love is always wrong, isn't it? Because if there isn't some kind of drama and dope involved, it's just too predictable. Why don't you start seeing that greasy actor you were so hot for, the one who shows up two days late for your dates? That's sexy, isn't it? That way you don't have to really express how sad or lonely you are. No, you can just listen to his fascinating stories about the script he's trying to direct and how he almost OD'ed and puked all over some agent's new Mercedes. Oh, that's fun, ha, lots of laughs, that's love, tenderness, certainty."

Angrily, Mia replies: "Wow, that's harsh. Why don't you just drop me off right here at Hadley's and I'll hitch a ride back into L.A.? You're fucking crazy. I just didn't dig the tunes, that's all. (She folds her arms and glares out the window.) I swear it sounds like something my mother would play really loud while taking me back up to boarding school. I don't need another fucking mother and, yes, maybe I will get it together with Vincent, because at least he doesn't try to get inside my head with all this crap. I wouldn't mind lying in his arms in some heroin stupor. That does sound hot, as a matter of fact, because you sure won't try it with me, which is a fucking drag. I love you so much, I really want to do that with you. It would be so beautiful; you'd understand it once we did it."

Leslie: "Oh, yeah, that would be just great for me, you must truly adore me. Here, honey, let me tie you off and shoot you up. No one's ever said anything so sweet to me before. It makes me love you down to the deepest part of my soul. Maybe we should stop at Hadley's. I could use a date shake just to recall my childhood, when I imagined something a little simpler in the way of love."

Where lips kiss mine
tender lips
dark on dark
the light would make you run away
predilection of love
who could know the direction
the trees may grow in the wind
in a place I had walked before
could I have possibly known this is where love would
    begin?
when you imagine playing with someone's heart
    that could push the buttons of a whirling wind
    that might stop and start around the post
this is only a test of my emergency broadcast system.

A Prayer

I see myself there and back again.
If the mirror is an illusion, then where am I now?
I can see both sides
but the reflection isn't mine.
If I believed you were the answer would I be with you
tonight?
I'm really trying to shake it all out.
You'd think I might know better by now
but it's easier to break a cast-iron skillet
than my old patterns.
I'm riding that edge.
The years seem not to make me any older.
Eliahu told me in another life I was a soldier.
I don't want to lose control
or reveal to you much more of my soul.
I realized that just the other day.
Onstage I tell you everything—I'm never afraid.
But in the middle of the night I write a different play.
Sometimes the only place I'm real
is like the movement of a clock I don't want to feel.
So I'm watching you now from the other side of the street,
wanting so to love you, be completely yours, so sweet.
But for now I'm riding that fine line
and until I can unravel it
I wait for a clearer sign.

Trucks floating down the freeway, not far from my house. But when I'm inside, I don't hear them. Big trucks with fancy yellow lights on top of the cab, beacons guiding them through the night.

Girls breaking up with abusive boyfriends. Smart girls who lost everything in the earthquake. Starting over, working out, not wanting to sleep with every guy who gives them a job. A *Silk Stalkings*, a spread in Australian *Playboy*. They dabble in Hollywood but would rather be anywhere else—on Prozac, gulping red wine, singing loud in therapy, cars and motorcycles, tattoos of panthers, a work in progress.

The 110, the 134, the 405, the airports and San Diego. Endless rivers of produce, gasoline, mattresses, power tools, tainted blood, girls blasting music, bawling behind the wheel. Home to studio apartments, unfinished scripts, the highways, the byways. Big dreams, silver wheels, lonely girls.

I can't hear any of them inside my house.

Although I never shopped there, the recent closing of the Broadway Department Stores in Southern California devastated me. I went to peruse the barren landscape of the Sherman Oaks store but found I couldn't stay long. The cosmetics department was wiped clean, with the exception of some Hugo Boss for Men cologne, Ultima II blushers, and a few assorted tubes of fruity body scrub. My friend Dana went crazy over the remains of crystal vases that boasted an additional 40 percent off the already low, low prices. It only made me shiver with melancholy. I left her in her reverie and headed over to hosiery, where I invested in white cotton and a pair of coffee-bean-colored Calvin Klein hose, both for $13.79. The saleswoman was vulnerable, and I asked her if she was sad that the store was closing. "Yes, I've made a lot of good friends here. This store is a hundred years old, even older. This store, Wells Fargo, AT&T. Fewer people serving more. I don't know who's going to take care of those computers." I guess the prices weren't low enough, and even the thought of Bloomingdale's taking over didn't console me. Why do these consumer landmarks mean so much? They serve as comfort zones, way stations on well-traversed routes, like some invisible hand holding us up. These bastions of consistency buoy us along life's seemingly unsolved journeys. I miss the landscape, even if I never roll in the grass. Clipping along at breakneck speeds, slowing down only to observe the disappearance of what usually appears as a blur in the background.

We can talk on the phone for hours late at night. Until I fall asleep. I'll let you think I'm your muse if it makes you feel better.

We can come up with a hundred ideas for movies and paintings and songs. You can freak out about your boyfriends, swear they won't be in your life. You can take them back and I'll be nice. It's all right if you come to rehearsal an hour late, drinking a Diet Pepsi, spaced out.

If you want to stir up some shit and make everyone nervous, I'll let you. If your parents still support you, control you, and you curse them, I'll listen and reassure you. When you run up a thousand-dollar phone bill calling the sex lines, I'll bite my lip and say nothing.

But when you crossed that line, turning your insanity into my reality, it scared you to see me walk away and be strong. If you had it your way, I'd still be under your thumb, believing that you created me in the first place, but I guess you have already discovered you didn't.

Dinner in the Valley at Mezzo Mondo. This chick walks into the restaurant. She arrives giving up major face and hair, a vinyl red platform, titties pushed up to the max, with an older guy—long hair and a low-heel demi cowboy boot. In the course of five minutes at the bar, this broad has given up more faces than Madame Tussaud's wax museum. One minute she's Edith Piaf, the next Bette Davis. She is a perpetual motion machine, mugging, bouncing, pouting, gesticulating madly. This guy is riveted; their wineglasses intertwine for a romantic toast.

So I'm driving around my old neck of the woods on San-dra Monica Boulevard between Fairfax and La Brea. First, I see to my left one of those pimply skinny hustlers wearing a pair of headphones, rocking back and forth by a bus stop giving up some *Boogie Nights* vibe. Then I look to my right and in some old broken-down white Toyota some chick with big hair is going down on some fat man, and I thought to myself, Get me the fuck out of my old neighborhood and get me some sage children. Purify this funky-ass mo-ment, this guy looking like Al Goldstein on Channel 35 in New York, a big fat Jewish shlub who obviously did not observe Yom Kippur getting head on Sandra Monica Bou-levard. The bitch was sucking his dick and then she sat up and they were laughing, looking over at me as if it was some kind of joke, but on top of that a really proud moment. It was as if they were taunting me, as if the actual act of having sex in front of the whole world wasn't enough—no, on top of that they had to be able to say "Fuck you" to somebody; to feel persecuted, indignant; like, "Here we are in the pri-vacy of our car being intimate and you penetrated our inner sanctum." And on top of that I actually felt guilty for driving past their "private" moment.

There are five helicopters midair on my way to the gym. Off in the distance, the 110 is backed up for miles, but I stay on it like a sheep following the crowd. At a certain point past Burbank Boulevard, there is no turning back—I am trapped by a holdup at the Bank of America on Victory and Laurel Canyon. I hang in there for an hour despite the warning of impending danger. The robbers are armed to the teeth with the deadliest of modern automatic weapons. The speculations fly and no one can speak of anything else. I fully expect to run into one of the criminals along the road as he takes me and my Acura Legend hostage.

It's an "emotional" house, Tanya told me as we drove up in her Cadillac De Ville sedan. She put out her minicigar in the ashtray and we proceeded in cautiously—real estate agents run the show out here in L.A. Don't waste their time, keep up with the pace, plan on taking care of a lot of the closing errands yourself. You're damn lucky to have someone get you the kind of deals they're pulling off for you, so don't ask for any extras, OK? Just be happy with the special qualities of that ranch house in Encino. Tanya was a tough chick and always kept the attitude that you would be buying the house one way or another. She looked a lot like Gloria Steinem, with aviator glasses and gabardine slacks. She sold real estate on the side but was really a screenwriter. And she was right: I bought the first house she showed me. That famous Spanish bungalow on Blix, I was guilted into it. After all, Tanya had taken the time to show it to me, hadn't she? So I'd damn well better have bought it. She sent me off to the escrow company. I didn't know what the hell I was doing. We celebrated by having dinner at a now-defunct health food restaurant on Ventura, where she loved the corn bread basket, because it was free.

It's L.A. It's October. And the crispness in the air—where is the crispness in the air?

I feel as I've never felt before, as if I'm standing on a precipice, at the crack of an open door. I feel my muscles sinewy and tight, as if I'm going to drive all through the night because I need to be alone just to rearrange my thoughts. Ooh, baby, I'm going to get into my car tonight, behind the wheel of my car, I'm going to listen to some music, some Neil Young, and drive real far. We'll spin all around this big beautiful town. I recall a time when you were feeling down. I took your little hand and I kissed it; baby, don't you know by now I've missed it? I know you're someplace on another coast, another country. I wish I could be free like you, baby, like you, baby. Tonight I'm going to get behind the wheel of my car and drive so far.

I feel very, very young tonight. I feel the way I did thirty years ago, maybe twenty. I feel I could fall in love again, the way I did when I was seventeen. I feel that pure, that clean—you know, no one's ever taken that away from me, that dream. I always want to be able to love like the very first time. Sometimes I pray to G-d at night to open up my heart, never close me down, never make me a cynic or take away my spark in the dark. I can feel all the love waiting for me out there. I can feel all the love out there tonight.

Tonight I'm going to get behind the wheel of my car and drive so far.

She said, lying in bed one day, "If I were a baby, I would just cry and cry and cry."

And I said, "But you're not."

And she said, "I know, and that just makes everything so much more complicated!"

Do babies dream in the womb? And if they do, what do they dream about? That the trees have spooky fingers?

Dancing out in the wind and the rain, they wave at her through the window. She closes the curtains, but their shadow reflects off the pane. The trees have spooky fingers, and even now she's counting the hands that swing back and forth and over and out, like clapping to a scary old band.

The trees have spooky fingers and she is all alone in her room, scratching and pointing like a railroad conductor when the train reaches the trestle too soon.

Good morning!
Morning, you arrived with no warning!
Upsy-dazy–lazy–mazy–crazy–snazy!
Good night, schluffy, little peanut in a shell, tonight
   you will sleep very well.
Roasty, toasty, and ready to dream, without the salt but
   lots of whipped cream.

I buy watermelon every day at the Korean grocery store. The woman who owns it says, "Oh, baby like watermelon, baby come soon." I get defensive. "No baby; no come soon; baby come in July." "Ya, you big; you know what baby is." "No, I don't know what baby is." I'm smiling, trying hard because it's New York and I know it's not easy for anyone, but this broad is tweaking my ass, every day—Korean groceries, salad bars, expensive fruit, overly interested proprietors.

Sandra, why did you have a baby?
To kill spiders and carry my bags.
A sign hanging in the rear window of my car:
BABY NOT BORED

This summer the spiders have been something out of a *National Geographic* special—more damn species than ever before. I think Miss El Niño stirred up the gene pool. There are some hairy ones, ones with armor, brown ones; some are translucent, speckled, sickly gray; some are dangling from the carport, pissed off, put out, spinning webs tougher than steel. It's a damn horror show.

There are always spiders in my house. They sneak in through the cracks and crevices. I don't know how else they could get in. They flatten themselves down and they slide in. Every night there's some spider trying to sneak into my room.

Old slick Mr. Jazzy Spider, top hat and a cane. "Hey, baby, I'm coming in for a little visit. It's late at night and you're asleep. I'll be climbing up your walls and making a little trip across the ceiling. Shoo-boop-doo-baa (scatting a scary little tune). Hey, down there; hey, little sleepyhead. What are you dreaming about, little girl? What crazy thoughts are going on inside your head? When I am ready, I will descend down upon a long, silken thread. Uh-oh, the air-conditioner is blowing me to the left, blowing me to the right—whew! Better anchor myself—yeah! Now I will come all the way down and bite you on your arm. Back up on the ceiling, I'll pull my web up from behind me (I like to recycle). Before you know it, I'll be back in the yard sitting in my web, picking my teeth, thinking, oh, you're waking up right about now, all panicky, shaky—'Oooooh I've got a big old swollen spot on my arm.' And you're thinking, 'Ooh, what's bitten me? Was it a black widow? Was it a brown recluse? Is my skin going to slough off? Will my arm fall off in the middle of the night?' I scare you, little girl, and I'm not even anywhere to be found."

Cool Lady Thousand
A new script I'm writing for Pam Grier.

Fade in:

A supersophisticated Afro-American woman is being sworn in by the Secret Service. She looks over her shoulder and winks at a sexy man; he nods and smiles. This is "Milly Williams," a kick-ass, in-your-face, buttoned-up cop turned superelite protector of visiting dignitaries. When she is assigned to guard a Saudi prince, all hell breaks loose. She gets in over her head, as the prince offers her the world and all she wants is an honest day's work and a cold beer at the end of it. She gets caught up and is forced to travel the world in a style she does not want to become accustomed to. Dior gowns, Dom Pérignon, Chanel No. 5, beluga caviar, and Learjets are just a cover-up for this pistol-packing mama. When an assasination attempt is botched, she kicks it into high gear, blowing everyone away. The prince begs her to stay; but with fierce pride, she looks him in the eye and says, "I could take your millions, but at the end of the day, baby, I'm just a cool eighty thousand." The prince, looking surprised, replies in astonishment, "I thought you said your name was Cool Lady Thousand?" Milly throws back her head and laughs. "Honey, that is what they all think. I am out of here!" The prince watches her board an Air Saudi flight back home.

I've put a new spin on an old saying, "I'll see it when I believe it." All the lies you told me—did you ever really mean them? I left a child behind just to hook up with you. I have almost lost my mind. Did you take me for such a fool? I cooked up so many delicious meals; I never brought you down or tried to make you feel unsure, insecure. No, no, no. Now I've got nothing left to show, so I'll be on my way home. I hope my baby still knows who I am. I hope my man will take me back again. It's not for lack of loving you, but you see I don't move that easily. I'll be caught with a cold wind on my mind. I cannot keep playing this one-sided charade. You stand there looking so sexy, and you think I've got it made!

I haven't got a clue, my friend. For all I know, the world stopped turning. I suggest that you just cast it to the wind; let it go, baby. Do you have a light? (Or something nice to drink?) Will you spend the night? (What do you think?)

Will you accept this collect call from somewhere in a small town in the pits of America? If you care at all. I just happen to be thinking twice; you know you haven't been sensitive or nice. But I must admit as I sit in this Greyhound, bring me down, look around, can't bear the sound. Hole in the wall, feeling so small, thinking of reaching out and touching a man—who, if he puts his mind to it, could be shy and gentle. Well, then, I could reconsider. Turn around and give it one more try. Aren't you going to try to stop me? Must I break down and cry?

Reckless, you're lost in time with no way to define all the people, all the parties. What should I wear tonight? Helpless, so you searched and you cursed, but it only got worse. Then you turn to me—baby, can't you see?

Poster for an Afro-American hair product on Eighth Avenue

Your man

My hair

His fingers

Your Drama.

After Natives

Like you, I've gone off on a big international jag. I'm an expatriate—it's rare that I'm here in the States now. I was not accepted, so I went to Paris. Along with all the other wonderful black divas of their times who were rejected here in America, I've been embraced and loved abroad; but of course I occasionally come back home, because I do become nostalgic and lonely for the good old days, the good old days. I always arrive late for my performances. The audiences expect me to keep them waiting. And I always do. It is the only way they respect you. I am an older and more seasoned woman than I was just a few years back, when I was green and naive. Not that I am jaded or tired. No, *au contraire,* when I step onto that stage and the spotlight hits me and my voice echoes in a concert hall or an intimate nightclub, I feel the way I did when I was a very young girl—giddy. But, child, when the night is through I must return to my hotel suite alone. It is a bit much, hanging up my gown and staring in the mirror at the reflection of the girl who once was and the lonely woman who is.

Today I watched *Splendor in the Grass*, with Warren Beatty and Natalie Wood. They turned it inside out, the shit was hot, and I was crying. You know those movies. We all think we're so sophisticated and they're so hokey they could never get to us. But by the end we're weeping: "I can't believe they didn't end up together." I couldn't even leave my house after that movie, I was so wrecked.

Just thinking about the way Natalie Wood died, I can't even drink this glass of water. (*Hasfa shalom, hasfa halela.*) Why, why did Natalie die? What was going on on that boat? There must have been some black magic going on, bat-wing, eye of newt. Somebody was stirring up the shit, because let me tell you, Natalie had no reason to climb over the side of that boat—except for some crazy voodoo happening, bringing her booty down into some rubber dinghy. Oh, honey, the moment was too sad. What about Natalie in *Bob & Carol & Ted & Alice*? Oh, honey, the bodies! She and Dyan Cannon had—ooh—turning-it-out titties, asses, fabulous sex! When sex was free and fun and you paid a price for it, but it was fun anyway. It was a morality play. Paul Mazursky once came to see me and sent me a letter: "Beautiful voice, hysterically funny, gorgeous, what more could a girl ask for?" How about a part in a Paul Mazursky film, for Christ's sake! They don't make flicks like that any-more—*Carnal Knowledge:* those carefree sexual forays before this false modesty or complete exploitation.

Warren Beatty called me the other day. It's so weird when I hear from him, because it'll be only once every three years. I'm like, "Why is Warren calling me?" And then I call him back and he says, "Where are you? What number are you at? Let me call you back." And then another three years go by and I won't hear from him again.

April Fools' Day, 1968. That's when I developed all my fantasies about international travel. Flying, before metal detectors, before Smarte Cartes. When Catherine Deneuve, holding a purse perfectly in the crook of her arm (not unlike Tippi Hedren in *The Birds*, who no matter how many times she had been pecked, maimed . . . , no matter how many heels had been snapped off shoes, the woman always had the handbag in the crook of her arm), ran traumatically and elegantly through that beautiful tunnel at the TWA terminal in New York, onto Ambassador Class. She sits by the window, crying, one tear falling gently. Looking out at the tarmac, at other flights taking off for international locations, to sophisticated places like Belgium. Sabena Airlines. Jack Lemmon comes in and drops a stuffed animal next to her. Life is perfect! And the service is divine.

Fade in/fade out:

Sandra Bernhard is taking a flight on American Airlines. She is tired, wearing khaki pants and tennis shoes. She's in Premier Class, but it doesn't quite have the sophistication of flights in the sixties. The stewardesses are older and offer her lobster claws as an appetizer. "I don't think so." A transcontinental flight for lobster claws—eyew! She tries to watch a movie on the tiny screen, maybe a Julia Roberts flick, but she can't focus. She falls asleep. Her head falls forward and back and to the side. She gets a crick in her neck and feels irritable and bitchy. Somebody sets before her a plate of goat cheese and grapes. She eats it ravenously and falls back to sleep again. She wakes to the smell of freshly baked chocolate chip cookies, or is it just that new canned smell of chocolate chip cookies?

"Miss Bernhard, we're descending into L.A. . . . Can I offer you a chocolate chip cookie and a glass of milk?"

"No, thanks. I'm all stuck together. . . ."

Why do I spend at least 25 percent of my time abroad figuring out what time it is back home? Sometimes in the middle of the night I'll wake up and think, "Well, it's three A.M. here, so that makes it nine last night in New York and six in L.A. So if I were in L.A., I might just be finishing my shower to go out for dinner. If I were in New York I'd just be ordering an appetizer; but here in Paris I can't sleep and I'm not even here."

It's over. The international journeys are not what they used to be. Stay home.

Bamboo in Ireland.
We walked all around Carton Demesne.
Me, Marianne, Patricia.
Winds whipping giant gray clouds,
wandering down the road with my eyes closed.
Never felt the air so light.
We talk about
the duchess who lived here, who built the place in the
    eighteenth century,
who bore twenty-one children with
her husband and then ran
off with the children's
tutor
and had three more
with him. She was still sexy, hot, being admired
by someone fifteen years her junior.
They grew fat but still sensual.
We eat our nonfat yogurt
and run on treadmills.
We walk
and there is bamboo growing in Ireland.

The swans
Come at sundown, preening, eating plankton, craning
   their necks.
Marianne calls out to their beauty,
so they come every day.

In Puerto Rico, insects left to their own devices will remain in one spot for days. On a recent vacation at a house we were renting, there was a grasshopper who looked as if he had been crossed with a lizard, stuck to a screen door; a green-leaf katydid resting on a terrazzo floor; and an indignant tarantula sitting petulantly in an abandoned fountain. The tarantula may have actually been dead, but the others were very much alive. Trust me on that!

Morocco is a dream.

The calls to prayer.

In the silence of predawn I sit up and imagine a world
without the luxury of endless needs and earthly
desires.

The calls to prayer are endless, like sirens.

Foghorn blasts cutting through the soul,

Reminders that we are unconscious, asleep, and numb.

Sitting in a courtyard of azure blue; cages of canaries singing in the afternoon breeze; beggars, veiled women, distant drums, and calls to prayer. Morocco is as I dreamed it would be and longed for it to be. I feel as if I have just left home for my first journey. There is something here that touches my soul. The dawn calls to prayer, shattering the silence and then echoing. I have cried and made new friends—unparalleled openness, kindness. When someone cannot give enough, time is compressed. Many worlds are working at once where I am and have been and shall be. *Bizathashem.*

We have been living it up in Morocco—Marrakech, the medina, hammom. Scrubbed by crazy, beautiful, full-figured gals. After an incredible dinner, an outrageous Ganawa North African band, henna tattoos at our new friend Ahmed's house, lit by candles until late into the night. I am lost in thought, feeling a spirit as if I had come home, reaching out, staying cool—a delicate balancing act of love and restraint against a backdrop of azure blue, faded sunset, orange, dreamy, dusty, smoky images of old love and new. How kind is the soul, the human touch, the word of a dear friend. I miss you and feel you here by the sea of Essaouira.

Maroc is a dream; the medina, the calls to prayer. In the silence of predawn, I sit up and imagine its world, without the luxury of endless needs, wants, and desires. I went to the grave of Avrahm Azuli, one of the greatest Kabbalists, who predicted the possibility of immortality in our lifetime.

Shabbat. Down a dusty alley to an azure-blue synagogue, the harmonies of Sephardic men below wrapped in ancient talit, just enough for a minyan. Snake charmers, anger, love, chaos, and peace—all of it a dream.

As if I have stepped into another time, here I am in Maroc. The smells, the images are as if from some dream or parallel life. I feel like I did when I was seventeen, traveling for the first time, young and seeing it all through the unjaded eyes of youth.

I know you would enjoy it here, the colors, the shapes of low mountains, the Berber nomads herding their flocks, dusty faded walls in the medina, smells as ancient and evocative as any on earth. The holy connection of existence not marked by time, space, or motion. Perhaps that is the purpose of ritual—continuity without explanation. We are fragile here on this earth, delicate threads holding us together, hands intertwined yet fearful. The sea soothes the love of mothers. Universal is the song of birds, tender and familiar the roundness of the earth and gentleness of song.

Here we are in this little modular city of the past, next to the sea in a courtyard from above. I watch you painting in sea-foam colors, washed by tears to perfection. You lie next to me, hand on my back, your foot extended over the side of the bed. The coolness of early night. I want nothing. I am here with you. Love, and not desire, rules my heart.

The calls to prayer are endless—like sirens, foghorn blasts of a taunting reminder that we are unconscious, asleep, numb. On straw mats they fall to their knees, prostrate bodies angled toward Mecca. Awaken, demons, and shake them loose, free, where they can roam or take possession of those less holy, connected, humble.

Mogador.

Tonight in an ancient city on top of a dark continent with sea and sand and wooden boats, men in peaked caps, crafts, wares, cannon turrets, tide pools, wind-shorn rocks blasted by time, deep breaths followed by strangers. I want to run, to fall into some madness—dangerous reckless shit that I never do. I could right now leave my room and wander alleys as if I didn't need anyone to hold me or tell me what is right or wrong. I want no direction or compassion or false love, but I stay here with candles burning and wait for silence to shatter, to come, to go to sleep tonight in a tender dream.

The police in Mogador.

"I arrest you, I fuck you, then I steal your jewelry, and you can do nothing about it!"

I could search the whole world for scents. Travel from medina to souk, collecting rare oils of amber, patchouli, sandalwood. Lost in a world of smells that take me back a thousand years in time.

Some essential oils you can't put directly on your skin, so I put them on my scalp, and when my head heats up it acts like a ceramic ring around a light bulb, and the scent fills the room.

Who will say kaddish for Uncle Herb?

I smelled the mixture of oils and cologne that emanated from him the night before he died. I was sitting on the edge of my bed doing the *ana bacoah* with my eyes closed, meditating for his recovery. He must have come to me, because his smell filled my head and my room, and then he left. Souls will reveal themselves sometimes. No one ever disappears forever.

I had my head buried in your shoulder so I could smell you, your salty sweat and dreamlike shine. When I lifted up, the moonlight came through the window. Your eyes were closed, wet, frozen, lost in a trance.

So I suggested a trip to the bedroom. I even took you by the hand—rings of silver and precious stones on several fingers, so I kissed those fingers that intertwined with my own and licked in between rare oils, possibilities of eternity. There we were on your bed, crazy winds blowing the lace curtains, night birds singing, fussing, fighting. I had your arms over your head and held them there, humming some sad little melody, familiar, haunting, reminiscent of your heart. You weren't forthcoming because things had happened before that you longed to erase. I cupped my hands over your face to heal you. No one could convince you that it would all just go away, broken and tattered, fragmented. You know, I tried to put it all together for you and, for a while anyway, it worked. Then I put a crown of leaves on your delicate head and breathed in the hot loveliness that emanated from there. You were everything to me. I can't imagine life without you. When you slept—peaceful, restless, tossing—I sat watching you through the smoke of darkness. It was hazy there, so I too longed for sleep. You've been gone now for some days. I try not to think of you every moment, though you are there constantly; and I miss you, wondering, tender, crazy. There was a message there that the rain smeared and the tears stained, but I didn't need to read it, having memorized it so long ago.

I tried to reach you on your cellular; you were out of the area. I left you a message on your machine. There were so many beeps that I thought maybe it was full.

Faxed you; paper jammed! You've missed a few, I guess. Couldn't log on to the Internet to send you an E-mail. Missing you.

Figured you might read this all these months later. Not even sure where you are at this point, but I love you as I always have loved you.

Phone Messages from André Talley

Monday, 8:38 P.M.

Hello, darling. It is Mr. Talley. We will pay. I want four of the best seats on December 2. Don't tell me you're not there on Tuesday. Manolo Blahnik will be flying in from New York on the second of December. Manolo Blahnik and myself, Mr. Malkamous and his lover, we want the hottest seats in the house. I want to be right there in the quiver of the heat. I heard you read Naomi to filth. I want to be right there to take in every single word about Ellen DeGeneres and all of them. You did not call me back last night. Are you having an affair? Were you eating pussy? Could you call me back? I'll call you at four in the afternoon. Still waiting for the call, darling. We will pay for the tickets; we want four of the hottest seats. We're not calling begging for handouts now, darling. Get it; get with the program; call me back."

Wednesday, 3:43 P.M.

"Darling, it's André. I guess the royal shoes have arrived for a royal artist. They are truly regal, and we love the thing in the *Post* today. But I know you just loved those shoes that Mr. Blahnik chose with tender loving care, and his special hand chose it with the special pom-pom of life. Give it up for those shoes; aren't they fabulous? Anyway, I'm exhausted. I feel lousy; my health is not as it should be; but I'm down here in Durham in my house with the trees, reading and realizing, reading this wonderful book by Jamaica Kincaid about her brother dying of AIDS. You've got to get it; it's very real, very personal. Hoping you're fine. And you should feel so high over your major, major moment; and I will never get over that spider, ever. I mean, it was moving me—chilling, gripping, touching, and Oscar Wildean. It was just fairy tale–like. You can call me, darling. If you don't have the number, you have to call the Couture House of Shoes to get the number."

Friday, 1:12 P.M.

"That's right, it's André. Oh, dear, here we are in a lovely part of the world called Paris, cold, gray, Frenchy, snooty, snotty, Camemberty; lonely—glamorously lonely, sparklingly lonely—but here we are! The tough went off, but I did give away a lot of shit. I gave away shit shit shit shit shit shit shit shit shit shit shit shit shit shit!"

High heels, at their most refined, are an artful tableau lying next to a stranger's bed.

I ran and ran in my heels and no one stopped me. How was it possible to be so vulnerable, weeping openly next to a subway stop—taking stumbling, aching, stilted little steps in my stilettos.

Big, fat legs tapering into slender ankles crossed on a couch. The slimming reflection of a pool of light bouncing off a snakeskin pump.

She stood for quite some time next to her car on a deserted highway. Standing all cockeyed, one perfectly clear plastic high-heeled mule adorned one foot, with the heel of the other mule snapped off, resting next to the tire. Resigned, shivering, holding the broken heel like a dagger in one hand, a purse resting in the crook of her arm. If danger lurked, no woman was more prepared.

A woman with a strong southern drawl buying Manolo Blahniks in London: "I'll take these three pairs. Do you think I need pads in these shoes?"

Her feet are not unlike a Cecil Beaton illustration.

Like Imelda Marcos, I kneel before my altar of soles. Here I light incense, tap a chime, chant mantras in hushed tones, drawing in all the energy and mysticism of the universe. There is perfection in the stiletto heel of a thigh-high Manolo Blahnik patent-leather boot. Balance and serenity in the delicately shaped toes of Mizrahi's suede Belgium pump. I inhale through one nostril and out the other as I meditate on a sleek Gucci T-strap. I am at ease in the world and ready to face the day. As I slip into a new pair of heels, I channel the consciousness of a Zen master. Where will my path lead me? At what point will my sole be worn? How many city blocks before it gathers a stain of grease, a wad of spit, a stray clump of earth? Who shall pass my way? An envious transvestite coveting my mules? A kind and handsome old gentleman, eyeing my feet with fond memories of a lost love? An ambitious young career girl embracing her decision to opt for the comfort of tennis shoes with her smart suit? I traverse so many lives. There are the strangers I pass and may never meet, and yet I step on pieces of their hopes and dreams, collecting them from place to place like rare jewels. All their karma is absorbed into one sole.

When I walk slowly, the heels are an endless connection to the earth around me. Thoughtfully, I step over streams of rain rushing into the street, the environment torn and bruised beneath my feet. I tread tenderly. I pause to brush an errant damselfly from the tip of a crocodile lace-up, moved that she has managed to find her home once again. I begin to run the rhythm of my heels, tapping out an SOS on the pavement, with all the hordes of humanity around me—suffering, celebrating, redeeming, hoping, lost and found. All are reflected in the shiny leather binding my feet, an unspoken promise, reflected back at me, life hanging in fragile balance. In awe, I step lightly, yet assuredly, with passion and fervor. I am all at once a humble student and an ascended guru—quiet, resolute, and spiritually aligned for my journey in the perfect heel.

Why do I insist on wearing those outrageous high heels?" I crossed my legs and admired the bulge of my calf exaggerated by the arch of my shoe. I stared down at her conservative little heel and boat-shaped slip-on, which gave her feet the illusion of floating away down a shallow creek like a withered fall leaf. I sipped on a sweaty scotch and replied warmly, "When I walk out the door in a good pair of heels—and I'm not referring to some kitschy crap that you can buy on a trip to Frederick's of Hollywood; but a really solid set of heels from Manolo or Prada, Chanel, Clergerie—I never feel vulnerable. There's no time for any weakness; I feel focused and strong on the corner hailing a cab. You'd better believe I'm the first fare he'll slam on his brakes for. You put the two of us just a few yards away, and he'll pass you right by. Why? Because I demand respect and my heels back me up. So don't go worrying about me; I've never been better. Care for a cigar?"

I'm out of here! I need to hit my streets and my stride in big, sexy, gorgeous stiletto heels—sharp as razors and deadly as vipers. If I choose to walk in Times Square at three A.M., the seas of danger will part. For no one, from the sleaziest pimp to the lowest thief, would dare to come near—the click of steel on concrete, the over-the-shoulder glance of total certainty, the light of protection reflecting off the tip of my sole.

The phone kept ringing on the thirty-eighth floor. It rang and rang in the office of Cherise Mantant. It echoed down the halls, masking the sounds of breathing and murmuring. Perhaps office hours were over, but sometimes a girl has to work late. This was one of those liaisons where no one removed anything at all, from silky blouse to giant patent-leather T-strap Jordans. Elevators were still as lights shimmered on the skyline. It was over quietly, and no one seemed to mind. I guess you could say it was a chilly affair.

Hey, Shoshana, bring me some Excedrin. My head is like a ripe fruit gone bad. I want you to massage my feet, hit some pressure points, release my demons!"

I sat on the floor next to her chaise longue rubbing rose oil onto her perfectly manicured feet. "Look, Sarah, Rebecca, Leah, if you want to do your people proud you'd best pull yourself together. What in hell are you thinking, you want to get a man? Please him, keep him satisfied. And stop hunching over like Quasimodo's stepsister. Hold up that head. Oh, now, don't hesitate and lead me to believe you are longing to lick some nasty pussy, PU, because I will not stand for that crazy shit. You are a lady, a protégée of Miss Ember, and the only pussy involved in your sexual future belongs to you. I draw the line and *dare* you to cross over. You'll never come, that's for damn sure.

"Now let us begin with the beguine. I know a fine young man, and I will be presenting him to you sometime in the next week. You will, as of tomorrow, start dressing the part. You clean it up—douche, scrub, freshen, squeeze, pick, probe, pluck, polish, file, tease, spray, moisturize, manipulate. Each day there will be a written and oral exam, so I suggest that you study, for I am not going to hold your hand indefinitely, *capish*? Holy Jesus, you just hit some point on my tender sole that has me ready to pass a stone. You've got the touch of Dracula. By tomorrow I want you to comprehend the meaning of caress. You go touching a penis like that and it could be grounds for domestic violence. All right, help me up. I am about to go to that magic place, where the lights will take me to the heights. Study Slenderella and let us move and groove!"

I was looking better and forcing myself to accept the concept of heterosexuality. If it made *her* happy, that's all that mattered. I dressed up and blew out my hair. I stopped hating myself and looking for excuses. I pushed up my breasts, squeezed into some heels, and lined my lips. When she introduced me to Michael, I extended a clean hand without a hangnail or dirt underneath the nails. He kissed it lightly, and a sense of calm swept over me, as if I were Jackie Kennedy greeting guests at the White House.

"Now, this is Michael Weinstein, he is one of your own kind, so you'll have plenty to talk about. He is my physician, so don't keep him up all night long with your fantasies and forays into show business, because he hears it all from me. Remember, that's my gig, child of milk and honey. Before you two disappear, I would like a complimentary exam of various and sundry bruises and slowly healing sores. Now, child, wipe off that look of wonder and high drama because I've got two shows tonight, and I can't be lifting your damaged spirits. Snap to it! Grease me into my Mackie and touch me up, recalling all my days of splendor and glory, which as you know have *only just begun*! *Voilà*! Gotta keep movin'. Gotta keep movin'!

As cool as it was to wear Chanel's Vamp nail polish, it is now so much cooler to just trash it and declare how *over* it is.

You know, she's become very spiritual."

"I can tell, her whole face has changed. She's so much calmer and more serene."

"I know, and I love her saris; they say so much about where she's been. Is she still funny? I mean, you really can't be so sharp and edgy and cutting and be spiritual, can you? I mean, that hurts people, which of course is in direct conflict with being a truly enlightened being."

"You know, you're so right about that, and come to think of it, she rarely speaks these days. When we had dinner last week—which was just a few bowls of rice and seaweed—it was hard to understand a lot of what she was saying. She was so soft-spoken and thoughtful. I said damn it once or twice, and she blushed. Well, yes, it's quite a big change for her."

"What do you feel like doing tonight?"

"Well, how about smoking a joint and grabbing a flick? Should we call her and see if she would be into it?"

"No, I think she's going to a big benefit for the Tibet House tonight; Natalie Merchant is singing."

"Wow, I really admire her; I'm such a loser."

"Oh, no, she would never want you to feel that way."

"I know, but I'm starting to, and—well—it's bringing up a lot of stuff for me right now."

"Maybe we should try to get last-minute seats for this concert tonight. That would make you feel better."

"No, that's OK. I'd rather hang with you and get stoned."

"I love you for that, and so does the universe!"

I know you were stunned into silence this evening. "Is that her?" It was a shocking moment, I know. It's OK; you're going to recover; we're all going to recover together. We're going to do what we have to do to get through this little experience, post–Rosh Hashanah, post–Yom Kippur, *bli-enera baruchashem.*

I hope your fast was easy. Mine was an amazing cleansing experience. I needed it, believe me; it was like a deep pore extraction for the soul. It was like a spiritual facial, squeezed, popped, steamed out. These moments are what it's all about—little moments, precious moments, moments that you want to savor and hold on to forever. That's what life is: a collection of rare and unusual moments, like an array of gems spread out before you.

Occasionally you open up their velvet cases and you gaze at them, even if you never wear them again. You gently finger one of them and remember the time that you wore it so proudly and felt so connected to its particular energy. But you moved on and you've cleansed and you've shed and you've carefully put your jewels back in a drawer that doesn't even lock because if they're stolen, the memory will suffice. It will be all right, I swear to Jesus Christ above.

I have no problem acknowledging the power of Jesus; it is no contradiction to me, even though every night I scan the Hebrew letter, the *Zohar*, the *Ana Bakoa*. I get deep down into a meditative state of Jewish spirituality, and I can acknowledge Jesus; and that is the beautiful reflection of no judgment, no fear of any alternative spiritual expression. That's where I've come to, and I wanted to share it with you.

We can all walk together very easily on this earth, because we're all from one soul. I know that may be a little bit heavy, but I think you can handle it. I'll get you believing and I will not be deceiving because I may be conceiving as we speak.

I woke up at three-thirty A.M. last night, as I always do. My internal clock, set on some intense spiritual time, goes off and I'm up. Well, last night I really wanted to be up to join Israel in bidding farewell to Yitzhak Rabin. I went to bed with volume fourteen of the *Zohar*, because my heart felt so shattered that I wanted to cover it with the book for protection and in order to send light back to other people who felt devastated. King Hussein of Jordan spoke in a way that brought the world to a new level of consciousness, so passionate and eloquent, really connected to the sadness and resolving to go on with peace and certainty. Leah Rabin was surrounded by her children and grandchildren; I imagined her the night before, alone in her bed, weeping, reaching out for her husband but finding no one. Is anything more unbearable than the thought of the person you adore, who supports you through the night—the person you balance against in sleep and dream—gone forever? And you think about the rest of your life in that condition, recalling every night you joined each other in that quiet place of intimacy and love. To talk about the day's events and the desires for the next day to come. It's as if you had become a raw nerve rubbed into a throbbing state of unbearable pain and loneliness. His granddaughter, with ginger hair, was one of the last to eulogize him. Oh, if words were ever more potent, if I've ever wept harder, I cannot recall when. She spoke of his caresses, and you felt the gentleness of a grand-father's touch. Imagine her curled up next to him, telling him something special and lovely. How he must have beamed with pride at such a pretty sweet girl, his flesh and blood, the future that he fought for, the tenderness contra-dicting the anguish of the outside world, the smell of home, the taste of a cold drink in a heavy sweating glass with melted ice. The embraces and laughter, fractured, wrapped in a shroud of linen growing cold; the ascending soul; the weight of the earth; the stars and the nearly full moon casting light on a fresh grave; all alone, starting on the jour-ney of spirit completed for this lifetime; the sounds of night, of silent Jerusalem, ancient keeper of all your sons and daughters, crisscrossing on various celestial travels. On these nights, can we even begin to think that we are not all con-nected? Dream meets dream in houses dark, with breathing and beating heart; no longer can we turn away from one another; each hope, each prayer uniting, forgiving, em-bracing the sweetness of struggle, the guidance of G-d and thankfulness for each morning bursting though the darkness and then the settling of azure blue over the sun, quieting this land, soothing it, protecting the ancient world. The bloodstained sheet of song, song of peace, it will lie folded four times, somewhere, where the heart rests and time reveals all.

We traveled back four thousand years, to the smell of incense and altars, sacrificial meats, letters of Hebrew whirling around my soul. Fighting death with bitter herbs, chewing until the bitterness turned to sweetness, seven hundred souls (as the snake venom cures snakebite), in the Beit Hamigdash in Jerusalem, before Sinat Hinam destroyed it; the purity of meditations, the cleansing of our inner *hametz,* crumbs of bread that connect to the ego, the desire for oneself alone; here we eat matzoh that draws mercy, that has no desire. No longer can we blame outside forces for our destruction, but with the power of unity and connection to the upper stratosphere we take control of our destiny. No more the ever-suffering victims driven away from our homes. But instead, strength and certainty with the love of our neighbors as ourselves, and the desire to receive for the sake of sharing. Our true New Year, Pesach, the binding of the ram, the control of desire and selfishness, with all of our friends in the courtyard of the Ari, ten times *eyen beit,* twice the light, ten times the seventy-two names of G-d, for we came only to make our corrections, our *tikune,* as we cleanse our souls in the *mikvah,* returning to the womb before our corruption. Every day brings that climb upward to righteousness, light, and *binah*-consciousness—through the *Zohar,* the power of the Hebrew letters, the acts of love, patience, and kindness that we must take out into the world, or none of this matters.

Germans invented Monistat.

On a recent late-night cross-country flight, I found myself seated next to the venerable actress, politico, and legend Vanessa Redgrave. Of course, I was quiet and deeply respectful, not wanting to disturb or intrude upon her. In fact, I immediately fell into the role of her dutiful servant, speaking not a word but anticipating her every need, desire, and whim.

As the plane rose into the dark night, she began arranging her paraphernalia, assorted Penguin Classics including *Hannibal's Battles*. She also turned over a page of a large yellow lined notepad and wrote across the top in large lettering "Antony and Cleopatra." I quickly looked the other way. We had yet to make eye contact or utter a word, and I remained in unspoken awe.

The flight attendants began their early flight duties, including offering beverages. Vanessa, braless, in an off-white silk blouse and without a stitch of makeup, ordered a Bloody Mary and resumed thumbing through her references and jotting down an occasional note on the yellow pad. She drank her Bloody Mary with gusto and then closed her eyes.

I went to the bathroom and came back to a deeply sleeping lady. I sat back down like a feather floating down from the air. I must have dozed for a while myself, and I felt her close to me as if we had fallen toward each other in a dream;

but I was afraid that if I opened my eyes it would break the magic connection between us that I knew could never happen again. When hunger overtook me, I sat up. She was staring out the window and I felt shy and awkward, and still not a word was uttered.

As I often do these days, I had brought myself a sandwich from Barocco. Unwrapping it carefully, so the tomatoes would not spill out, and holding it close to my mouth, I began eating with great relish and joy: a fresh, lovingly prepared turkey on whole wheat with organic mixed greens and a sprinkle of oil and balsamic vinegar. Now I became aware of Vanessa glancing over at me, and I was excited because I swore she was ready to break the ice and strike up a deep conversation, but still I kept my eyes straight ahead. She was feeling around the side of her armrest and then, finding the proper button, signaled for the flight attendant to come over, which he did posthaste. Looking up at him, she rather commanded, "I'll have one of those," pointing at my sandwich. He looked down uncomfortably and responded, "Oh, I'm so sorry, Miss Redgrave, but I believe the young lady brought this herself." Everyone fell quite silent until I finally apologized to her. "If I'd only known that I was going to be traveling with you, I would have brought you one. Would you like the other half?" I think I might have almost cried out when I said it, but she rather tersely rejected my offer. Crushed and confused, I ate as much of the other half as I could while Vanessa snacked lightly on smoked salmon and caviar aux blini.

I studied the lines in her face, the angle at which she held her hands, the line of her neck, the etches of time, memory, life lived; and as we touched down on the runway at LAX, I finally managed to let her know in the fewest possible words how much I admired her work and her commitment to her beliefs. "Thank you," she said. I hesitated. Thinking twice, I leaned over and put my arms around her, kissing her on both cheeks. She tried to pull away, but it all happened so quickly that it was over before it began. I tried to say, "I love you," but the words got caught in my throat and stuck there. I ran off the plane crying. Fortunately, there was an abandoned Smarte Carte waiting for me as I exited. I didn't look back, although I knew she was there, still stunned and completely turned off.

Well, it's Christmastime again. Last Christmas didn't work out so well for me. I was with someone, feeling a little impatient and jumpy with the season. I made a mistake and next thing I knew, they were gone on Christmas Day. Before I could say anything, the holiday moment was over. I took myself to the movies—*Shine*—and then out for a Chinese lunch. "Peking duck, missy?" "No, thanks." I walked back out onto the abandoned streets; there was no snow or any sign of holiday cheer. I wanted to feel the cold, but the weather just hung there as uncommitted as an affair with a married man. I found an open bar and cozied up to a couple who were three sheets to the wind. I ordered a Rémy Martin and belted it back. The pope was on television delivering his message of peace and harmony, and twinkly lights illuminated the Christmas tree. I fixated on the bartender's veiny nose—Rudolph had nothing on this guy. I was walking home looking for a gift to give myself, but I realized then that I had everything I wanted. My lover called and said, "Why don't you get on a plane and meet me?" I replied, "I love you, but I think I am going to sit this one out." Is there anywhere in the world that feels magical on Christmas? Is there anyplace that doesn't feel like Christmas at all? This one was feeling somewhere in between, and there was no place to run or hide.

I keep trying to remember to tell you about something really important; it keeps slipping my mind. Oh, yeah; I know what it is: "The Forgotten Woman!"

Irene managed them all, Lily, Chita, Lana, Esther Phillips. Every new town they would pull into, Queenie—Esther's sidekick—and Esther would go to Saks and try on gowns for that night's performance, somehow managing to walk out with a fabulous new ensemble for each show. One night in Detroit, Irene took that night's kitty in cash. She left the club, and Esther's gang held her up at gunpoint and stole the money and, according to Irene, gave it to Esther so that she wouldn't have to pay commissions. Irene lived large, and often I would buy her fresh new outfits at Lane Bryant. She once invented a turkey wing and apple diet; and she would often get extreme and go on Optifast, slimming way down.

When Irene entered my life it was from stage left, it was as if a whirling dervish had spun some kind of mad tapestry around me. We went on the road in rented cars—myself, Brian (my keyboard player), and Irene behind the wheel. She wore many hats, from bellboy to producer. She loved the lights, "so many lights." She operated the sound board and critiqued my vocal stylings. We always shared a room on the road; two queen-size beds and a rollaway for Brian. I would sleep facing him all night, afraid to see what Irene might be up to.

Oh, there were some nights, like the one leaving Hampton Beach, New Hampshire, on our way to Burlington,

Vermont. The motel had packed us a midnight picnic, as we had left after the show. Brian and I were overwhelmed by the sight of the northern lights performing; "Pull over, Irene," we screamed gleefully, and ran down a hill to witness one of nature's greatest spectacles. We were completely caught up in it when we realized that Irene was missing. Had she been eaten by some wild beast? But much to our shock, she had remained in the car, the light illuminating her frenzied attack on the fried chicken and sticky pecan buns.

In Burlington, while onstage, I asked for a cigarette from an audience member, and a beautiful young University of Vermont student named Janice Cable ran up from the back of the audience to bring me one. She created quite a spectacle, and she came backstage after the show to offer her services, which were eclectic and enticing. While Irene was settling the books, Brian and I headed back to the 'Round Towner and locked the door. We put Randy Crawford in the ghetto blaster and cranked it up. Janice put on an exotic dance performance that blew our minds and ended up in bed with Brian (although she wanted to be with me) performing a high-wire act, which was punctuated by a loud knocking on the door. When we realized that it was Irene, we told her to go find another room; it ended up in an ugly confrontation between the two of us in the hallway. "I want that girl out of here immediately," Irene screamed in her high British accent. "No way, Irene; Janice stays! Now go to bed!" She was as red as a beet and didn't speak to us again until Connecticut, where she snuck out for fried clams—which I promptly threw into the Dumpster, trying to keep her on some semblance of a diet.

When we weren't on the road, things were a little bit more mellow, and she was happier at home with her five cats, who also enjoyed eating. We parted ways when I discovered that I did have to pay taxes, despite the fact that she had assured me that once you incorporated you never had to pay them again.

Another Scene from an Indie Film

Girl in bed asleep. Someone, presumably her boyfriend, is trying to rouse her. Girl: "No, no, honey, five more minutes. I have to finish this dream." Boyfriend shrinks away and gently closes the door as the Wallflowers sing something heavy. They go to the Best Western coffee shop for a late breakfast. The girl sees someone she's trying to avoid who comes over; the girl's sunglasses are on her head as she leans against the booth. She is fucked up, hung over, and cranky. The guy sits next to her, seriously concerned: "Are you OK? I ask Amanda about you all the time. We haven't seen you at any of the meetings lately, so we start to worry. You know, I mean you look good, but we just want to make sure!" She's pale and annoyed: "Oh, yeah, sure, I've never been better. I'm going to Rhode Island to star in a movie, so when I come back I'll call you and come to a meeting. I'm cool." "Well, that's great because you look good, but we just worry." He kisses her cheek and goes back to his booth. She downs an orange juice and smiles weakly at her boyfriend, who appears depressed.

OK, so you don't want to be caught sitting in the living room looking like a geek. You know she's on her way over and you need to play it cool, so you decide to hide out in the kitchen with all the blinds drawn, typing something. Anything to appear preoccupied and kind of oblivious, because that's going to be your first fatal mistake, showing that you really care; because to care is to be sober and completely present, not strung out or self-absorbed. It means that you might actually be there for her, emotionally available. If you can just pull off the hard-edged motherfucker for a couple of weeks and lure her in, you might stand a chance. But if you show your hand too soon, you might as well forget it, because for sure she'll dump your sorry ass so fast and hard you won't know what hit you.

Russell Simmons' Def Magic Jam.

"Get in that box, bitch; I'm gonna cut your mother-fuckin' ass!"

The Weather Channel—who told you about it first? You were so resistant, so jaded, but then the floods came and the great winter of 1996, and who was the first person you called? "Hey, what channel did you say the Weather Channel was?" So don't pull that. It was me who discovered it first, shit, so don't pretend you're on the cutting edge of pop culture or something, because you and I know the truth!

The Weather Channel—A Slow Day

There were no fronts today. Nothing. Zip. Nada. Over in Oklahoma it rained for a few minutes, just a piss in the wind. We're all cranky as hell around here; can you blame us? The sun is shining, it's warm; well, you can just go ahead and enjoy yourself on your own; we're out of here. When something comes up, we'll be back. Any sign of nature rearing her ugly head, we'll come right back on, but until then go ahead and enjoy this beautiful weather—it sucks!

We're waiting for a tornado, a flood, a hurricane, an earthquake. Until then we'll just keep it real quiet, OK? We'll be right back with the five-day travel planner. What a bore!

The Discovery Channel teaches you how to reattach bowels and perform open-heart surgery.

Deals in Development: *The Hollywood Reporter*

Patti Smith to play an aggressive businesswoman who started a little late in the game, has a flirtation with the CEO of the company she's trying to aquire by hostile takeover. Slated for midseason replacement on CBS.

Marianne Faithfull playing a kooky English expatriate married to a man who manages a trailer park with a racist cop brother-in-law. Fox is looking for a place in their fall lineup.

Stevie Nicks copilots a 747 for a large airline on an international route. Each week caught up in another harebrained situation: hijackings, women giving birth, people smoking in the lavatories. She's high flying and problem solving on this NBC hit comedy.

Just when you think you have seen her do it all, Camille Paglia takes on the game-show circuit, in this brainteasing new Merv Griffin production of your favorite childhood game, *Twister*. In syndication, covering 180 markets.

Isaac Mizrahi and James Brolin in *Pit Stop*. Quinn Martin is back in the game with this brawny look at funny-car racers.

I'm noticing a very disturbing trend toward people obsessing over animals' behavior. Animals fighting, fucking, eating, acting just like people.

Hi, I'm gay. What do you do?"

At the recent opening of Planet Hollywood in Beverly Hills, California, I let loose and fell into the party spirit with some of the greatest luminaries of our time: Arnold and Maria, Bruce and Demi, Roseanne. Cigars were stoked up, logo jackets were well broken in, modeled on Sly and Jim Carrey. Limos ferried us all around the corner, less than a block away, to a long red carpet lined with fans and worn-out paparazzi blinding us with flashes. Down at the end of the walk was a big stage where different stars got up and talked about how momentous and thrilling it was to be here at the opening of the hometown Planet Hollywood. Silver platters of hors d'oeuvres and cocktails swooped around us.

I heard a lot of promises being made, offers of teaming up surprising combos of stars for film projects, hush-hush gossip, and loads of flirting. Oprah was grabbing people left and right, glowingly heaping praise on some of our favorite stars. I stood by and watched, trying to catch Oprah's eye— which, by the way, was adorned with catlike contact lenses that at once amazed and frightened me.

Well, finally my moment arrived. She looked over and threw open her arms, and as I rushed over, ready for her embrace, cutting right in front of me was none other than Cindy Crawford, who apparently had been the one Oprah was greeting, not me. Well, I was totally humiliated and saddened and what had started out as a big glamorous night for me ended in heartbreak. I walked away, crushed and crestfallen. Even the fabulous gift bag couldn't lift my spirits.

Beverly Hills Sightings

Nina Blanchard and Chuck Connors.

Nina with very Harold Robbins vibes, although maybe she had represented Chuck when he was on the super DL, rumored to have shown his weapon in a fifties gay porn flick. This was before he became the Rifleman.

There's nothing worse than feeling dumb and having millions.

First it was Evita the woman; then came the legend; now *Evita* is a major motion picture and a fabulous fashion concept at Bloomingdale's!

Far be it for us to dictate your fashion sensibility, but isn't it time you stepped into someone else's shoes?

You've been shy, a wallflower, afraid to express yourself, but now with a little coup from Estée Lauder and Bloomie's you'll be transformed into a heartbreaking icon around the house.

No more mousy brown retro shag haircut; throw out that studded acid-washed jeans ensemble. You'll be in total control with lacquered blond hair, pencil-thin eyebrows, gorgeous flame-red lips. Slip into a cinched-waist padded-shoulder suit so tight, you'll barely be able to move—don't worry, you won't have to. With the whole family suddenly on their knees, you'll feel like an empress surrounded by commoners. Your days will be jam-packed with excitement. Seduce an old friend or the whole damn neighborhood. Start a little controversy and turn it into a revolution. Remember the effect you'll have every time you walk into the mall, pull into Burger King, pick up a quart of milk at 7-Eleven; the masses will weep, throw themselves at your feet, dedicate their lives to you. You can erase that tawdry past forever with just a wave of your gloved hand and a trip to our exclusive Evita boutique at all our Bloomingdale's stores. Go ahead, let the public adore you; after all, you're everyone's favorite first lady!

Don't cry for us, Ms. Argentina. If you should suddenly grow bored or weary with that role, we have options. Here are just a few of the upcoming biopics featuring other fascinating ladies. Here's a sampling of upcoming personas you'll be clamoring to try on!

Other Biopic Fashion Tie-Ins

Mother Teresa: Look in Bergdorf Goodman for the no-nonsense simplicity of Mother Teresa's summer look—light starched cotton midknee dresses, the new length that all the girls are talking about, and those who aren't are just plain green with envy. Don't think you can just walk out of the store without a whimsical wrap for the head. A well-defined eye and an understated lip are in keeping with the good common sense of Mama T.

Well, you were waiting, and here it is, the rage of Calcutta. Don't forget, a rubber-wedge orthopedic shoe is the only thing to finish off the whole picture. You can find it all in our exclusive Giving It All boutique on four. Now you don't have to travel to India to feel like a saint; you can do it all in your own backyard, right after martinis and a nap. Grand opening of flick and boutique when the heavens above decree.

"The Embargo Is Over":
The Raghad and Rana Hussein Story

The brave new film that has all of Baghdad in an uproar, the real story behind Saddam's ballsy daughters. Sofia Coppola gives a star turn as Raghad; Winona Ryder is edgier than we've ever seen her as the brooding sister, Rana. It's a tour de force for everyone involved—a must-see for anyone who wants to go home again.

Looking to spend the night alone with your man, but Dad won't let you? Ready for a little sacrifice and a few wars? Well, you've stirred up a few in the past—why not take it all the way this time?

That's right, Barneys New York and François Nars cry, "Don't hide behind your chadors any longer!" Liberate yourself and step up to the breezy comfort of a thousand Arabian nights. Of course, when you simply long to watch without being seen, François gives you that big, glamorous smoky eye with accompanying beauty mark. You'll save a bundle on lipstick, too. Black is always au courant; from head to toe, layers and layers of Prada silk fall sensually in any direction you take them. One look works from day to night—great when you're on the run.

You've read about them, watched them on CNN. You'll be riveted by this touching family drama. Don't you dare try to escape; but if you do, remember there's no turning back. Your gift with purchase—a Gucci canteen, for those desert excursions—is limited, so please come early. Salaam! From Barneys New York.

Indira Gandhi: Sari Is All You Have to Say?

There's turmoil in the air. The tortured masses have taken to the streets. All the answers rest on one woman's shoulders. What do we say? Caste your fate to the wind. You've always been fascinated, wondered what drove her. These are the lives and times of Indira Gandhi, and now you too can walk barefoot in the Ganges, crush an uprising, and do it with the same elegant flair as Indira. Neiman Marcus proudly presents the Star of India boutique in conjunction with Merchant-Ivory films. All the gals will be clamoring to learn the secrets of wrapping; our patient Brahmans will take you deep into a meditative state. There you'll process a kind of inner peace you never dreamed possible. Chanel channels the simple earth tones you won't want to leave the house without. At Neiman's, all the scared cows simply evaporate. By special invitation only.

Now you too can proudly wear the Kennedy pearls. Yes, the exact same replica of the triple strand she wore while adorable John-John pulled on them. You will be able to feel the serene feeling that comes with not only possessing complete control but being so beautiful as well.

Yes, I'm wearing Jackie Kennedy's faux pearls, and I feel fantastic. This isn't simply any necklace; these triple strands evoke the feeling of racing through the ocean on my private yacht, the smell of manly sweat, the murmurs of someone cheating, puffs on big cigars, the laughter among men after the telling of a dirty joke. I'm soaking up the sun, lost in my dreams. Oh, yes, I am a content lady of leisure, and yet nothing can shake my foundation. Tomorrow I'll be jumping the horses, lunching with the girls, swinging the children through the air, all the while protecting them from the harsh realities of the world. I'll smoke in private and whisper sexy secrets in my quiet, charming, and seductive voice. My man may play the field but he always comes home, and that's all that matters. I like being alone. I love to read a huge tome while sipping a cocktail, closing my eyes and drifting away, jumping up to be coiffed and oh so perfectly coutured, the strains of a cello whirling about the dance floor, remembering my French, charming the guests and my man. These are my pearls! My baby pulls on them. I throw my head back and laugh. Wouldn't you love to join me?

I did not attend the opening of the Fashion Cafe, although the idea intrigues me. What can one expect to find? An amazing array of fascinating memorabilia? A set of Naomi Campbell's dirty G-strings? Claudia Schiffer's Koran-inspired dresses by Karl Lagerfeld, along with the original death threats from Arab fundamentalists? Perhaps there is a Tiffany display case of glue-on moles worn on the upper lips of Cindy Crawford and Nikki Taylor. You won't want to miss the beautifully mounted ticket stubs of Christy Turlington's nonstop flights on the Concorde. You'll be able to experience the endless hair color changes of Linda Evangelista in the café's exclusive Wash In, Wash Out booth. Take home the *Stay Out All Night Drugging, Partying and Sleeping with Whoever You Please and Still Wake Up Radiant* video. There's the Hall of Echoes: makeup artists trashing girls behind their backs, vicious fights on exotic locations between Veronica Webb and any younger, prettier girl. You'll be enchanted by Kate Moss's guitar stylings and marvel at how effortlessly Elle MacPherson makes the jump from simply staring into a camera to actually speaking to one.

The menu is simple, mainly consisting of a carrot stick or two with garnish. But for those not faint of heart, there's the binge-and-purge plate complete with a banana split for dessert. Instructions for putting your finger down your throat and making yourself puke are your take-home bonus!

For the guys in the crowd, you can experience rejection by bitchy fledgling modelettes posed strategically around the bar. They'll smile at you, you'll buy them a bottle of Cristal, and then they'll blow you off for an ugly but rich European playboy.

That's right, it's nothing but glamour and crazy fun with the edgy sexy troika every night. Why, of course Naomi, Claudia, and Elle will always be on hand. What could be more important than welcoming you to the home of international excitement and those super-duper models, at the one and only Fashion Cafe!

Rebecca Romijn says that the three most difficult parts of modeling are: traveling, adjusting to the time differences, and negotiating. It's very taxing. "You know, when I fly on the Concorde it takes three hours to get to London, where it's five hours later, so do I set my watch ahead two hours? And when I fly on Virgin Atlantic, it takes five and a half hours, so do I set my watch ahead ten and a half hours or only thirty minutes? I'm exhausted just thinking about it."

Someone Studying the J. Crew Catalog

Oh, are you ordering those fabulous new cargo shorts?"
"No, I'm picking out my next lover."

In big, broad strokes, the whole thing was a major fuckup. He hadn't spoken to her in a while, and everything was rash and without any concern for the reality that it was completely over. Well, I can say all this because he was my best friend. We worked together, smoked cigars, fucked some of the same girls. Well, OK, it was bordering on incestuous, but it worked. "Mike, you're a schmuck, but I love you anyway!" We were taking a trip to Miami—investments, bimbos, Cuban food, something sexy, hot nights. I was wearing Armani, and I needed to just be in some boxers, scratching my balls, belting back an ice-cold martini. If everything went my way, some chick would magically appear and *blow me*. You see, for my money, love was a big waste of time. The less I know someone, the better. The faster I come, the quicker she goes. Mike got suckered in and suffered for it every fucking time. Not me. I'm free of all the guilt, so I sleep like a baby and move like the wind. I'll try in my own way to bring you up to speed, but it's a story I don't want my mother to know.

Mr. D's Chinese restaurant on Eighth Avenue plays a lot of funky music. The other day, over kung pao chicken, Celine Dion performed her inspiring theme song from *Titanic*, not only the radio version, but a very up-tempo dance arrangement as well. By the third go-around, Steven and I politely asked the waiter to change it to something else. "You no like the song? Everyone likes song *Titanic*!" Not wanting to insult him, we simply explained that perhaps hearing it once might suffice. What I really wanted to do was scream and turn off that fucking song before I sank a ship myself.

And if there were a ship to take over the mantle of the *Titanic*, what would it be? What about the entire Carnival cruise line for starters? Have people lost their minds? Can someone possibly think that sitting out on a stinking, floating Vegas hotel for five days, running into the same people all day, could be interpreted as a vacation? Waking up in a cabin the size of a closet?

People like to hear the same song a thousand times and they like to sleep in small spaces on vacations.

There is a cruise ship out in the distance, all lit up at night. People are whooping it up, having so much *fun*! I'm talkin' Kathie Lee Gifford kind of fun, the kind that involves shakin' and drinkin', screamin' and laughin'. I bet right now there is some super-duper floor show just kicking into high gear, where the passengers—who at this point have all found special friends to bond with—are riveted by the shenanigans taking place on some rotating, floating, bloated stage out there right off the coast of St. Thomas. Where after a full night of entertainment, eating loads at a buffet, dancing to a live disco band, and stepping out onto a glamorous deck, and finally falling into a delicious sleep, lulled by the slapping waves in a capacious stateroom, the entire shipload of passengers will be disembarked to shop for tennis bracelets and a million other wonderful gifts from Little Switzerland. For six hours, they will be exposed to real people in native situations that can be tolerated only for an afternoon because, after all, coming from the sanitized world of Carnival Cruise Lines, one might be thrust into culture shock at the sight of people living such an exotic, scary, culturally confusing life as people are inclined to live out there.

No one wants to have to face that on a vacation, for Christ's sake. One wants all activities planned from sunrise to sunset, filled with the familiar sounds, smells, and language of home. Who cares if the entire experience has been sucked dry of any of the emotion, sensuality, or uniqueness that normal travel involves? As a matter of fact, the less you have to think about, the better. No one wants to be reminded of the fragility, loneliness, inspiration, and spontaneity of freewheeling travel in places with people one may never encounter in one's own backyard. It's easier this way—to go home with memories that don't wake you up in the middle of the night and make you long for an experience that could never be duplicated again no matter how hard you try. When the danger and possibility of all emotion are removed, then we can simply look forward without any change to our hearts, and people like that. They like to be cooped up in tiny rooms where windows don't open and the atmosphere is controlled. They like to hear the same song over and over, like the theme from *Titanic*. Celine Dion with a dance version of tragedy. It's comfy and neat, and no confusion is involved. Isn't it great to sail the seas and have everyone the same? Boat + romance − iceberg = *Love Boat*. In the meantime, all the dreams have sunk to the bottom: rusted, broken, and resting in the dark.

I love New York; it's such a constant parade of the strange and the beautiful. Not so long ago I was at this divine restaurant called Bond St. for sushi. When I stepped into the ladies' room to powder my nose, I encountered one of the most stunning older women I have ever seen. Although her face said fifty, I later found out that she was ninety-three. Needless to say, I was peering into every mirror, trying to catch a glimpse of the many scars she must have had from all of the nips and tucks—but not a single scar! The secret, it seems, was in her Godiva-like hair. Literally. It was all pulled up into a white-silver ponytail that stopped at mid-back. What the eye could not see, and only her confidants knew, was that the tail was held in place by a very high-tech bungee scrunchie. Each night she would rig herself up to a hook in the ceiling of her bedroom and hang by the scrunchie—thus pulling her face taut. In the morning, she would simply push the scrunchie down to accommodate the excess skin accumulated during the night and go on about her day. The frightening part is that inside all of that hair in the ponytail is years of stretched and pulled skin. One unfortunate snip of the scrunchie and upwards of seven and a half feet of skin would come rushing forward toward her face and puddle in her lap like a Mummenschanz clay face. I really admire that woman. Risking humiliation every time she steps out the door, knowing that danger could befall her with the snap of a single elastic band. What a trouper! I was so inspired that I ran home and experimented with collagen.

I'm from New York, so you can't impress me with some jazzy crème brûlée that you think you invented just because you tossed eight measly blueberries on top of it. Give me a strawberry-rhubarb pie. Give me an apple crumble with a scoop of homemade vanilla bean ice cream. And please don't try to win me over with your pretentious potatoes. I don't want some garlic mashed potatoes, or bacon horse-radish mashed potatoes, or wasabi fuckin' potatoes, for Christ's sake.

Here at Café Rosso I spend some of my most wonderful evenings, in deep conversation with the greatest artists of our time. We sit late into the night over bottles of Chianti and smoldering cigarettes, carrying on a passionate debate over the state of fashion, politics, art, music. One would imagine this to be like Berlin in the thirties or some dark basement in Franco's Spain. This is our lifeblood, our connection, not only to each other but to the universe, to our souls.

Come with me to this table, where I sat with Marlon Brando just days before his appearance on Larry King. I myself thought his ideas risky. "Marlon," I screamed. "Yes, I understand, but will Hollywood? You have the luxury of really delving into it here with me, but you know Larry—it could all go through the roof. Just think about it, that's all I ask!" But of course he is so impetuous, and it blew up in his face. He called me late that night and wept about the whole thing. What could I do but console him?

Right here at this table one crazy night Kevyn Aucoin plucked my eyebrows. It was mad. He pulled out his tweezers, which he never leaves behind, and grabbed my face: "Darling, I can't stand it anymore; I have to give you that perfect arch." Someone put on *Bolero*. It was very dramatic; no one spoke; we all held our breath. Of course it was painful and I was nervous, but I trusted

Kevyn, for he is the master. When the last hair was removed, he held up a small gold mirror; I stared at my new face and tears ran down it. A round of applause broke out. We all smashed our glasses against the wall and toasted in Russian. The dancing did not end until the first light of morning broke through the sky.

Did I tell you about my dinner with Antonio and Melanie? It happened soon after they began their affair, and it was uncomfortable and confusing. Between you and me, when Melanie went to the ladies' room, Antonio slipped his hand onto my thigh and began kissing my neck. "Jesus," I cried out, "what in the hell are you thinking? Isn't it enough that you broke your wife's heart, but now you're away from your new lover only two minutes and you can't control yourself?" His eyes were flames. "It's only a matter of time before you understand, darling!" At this point Melanie returned, and the conversation meandered from wild animals to Hitchcock. All in all, a rather stressful evening.

Gabriel García Márquez was puffing a big Havana cigar and devouring a plate of pasta. "Sandra"—he looked up at me with his mournful gaze—"when I sit here with you I feel like a robin's egg. So fragile, so translucent, full of life and the craziness of youth. I wonder to myself: Gabriel, are you jealous or sad because all these times have disappeared like leaves on a rushing stream? You represent, to me, first love untainted, rare. But you can see that I am an old man and ask of you things that you could not possibly understand; only the ravages of time will bring on the comprehension of loss and loneliness. Here are my few pleasures that remain: a glass of claret, a good cigar, a plate of peasant food, and the rare beauty and innocence that radiate from your soul."

He wept, and I held him. We talked for many hours as his cigar dwindled down into one long, perfect ash. I wanted to blow it into the wind, but I left it smoldering as we walked into the still of the night.

I wish you had, but I'm glad you didn't.

The Other Woman

I need a Manhattan, because this is a Manhattan story. I met a gorgeous man strolling down Madison Avenue. A sixty-five-year-old pilot for Air New Zealand. We started chatting. He was in town for a layover. Laying over me. And we began a ten-year affair at someone else's expense—his wife's. Have I told you about the time that we drove out to JFK in his rented Volvo station wagon? We pulled out onto the tarmac and made love while the jumbo jets were flying over us. I lost my head. And gave it too. I would have given up everything for that man. He's now flying the Asian route, and I hear through reliable sources that he's taken up with a pretty young thing in Bangkok. So you can only imagine what it must be like. It's not easy. And it's damn lonely, too.

I stayed single all these years for selfish reasons, to be available at all times for my men—and there have been plenty. There was François, the Swiss investment banker; Arnon, the Israeli orchestra conductor who was a gunrunner on the side; Ricardo from Buenos Aires, who turned out to be an SS officer. (He was sooooo cruel!) But at the end of the day, they will always go back to what's safe and predictable.

You would have thought that I might consider a way out, but not me. I love the simple things in life: the tulips blooming along Park Avenue in the spring, watching the waves crash off the coast of Nice, and stepping through the Acropolis—that always picks me right up. I have girlfriends who've taken pills to escape, stood on their balconies contemplating jumping off—way too much drama for my taste. I would rather take the Concorde to Paris and take a champagne bath at the Ritz.

Why would one ever contemplate ending it all when there are so many fabulous men to take your mind off the heartache? I chose this lonely life; I don't recommend it to everyone.

A woman is nipping at our heels on Jane Street. "I'm sorry," I say, "would you like to pass?" Crazy now, as if her life was in jeopardy: "I'm on my way to the *theater!*" Well, as it turns out we were all going to see *Hedwig and the Angry Inch*, so when we arrived right behind her only to find her waiting for a friend, we looked away—saddened for her, really.

Ever since I stopped using aluminum-based deodorants, my life has become a stinky affair. I figured that it was better than developing Alzheimer's when I'm seventy. But now that I reconsider, I think maybe it would be better to smell good while I'm young, so that I can find a mate to care for me when I develop Alzheimer's. As opposed to stinking all of my life and dying smelly, alone, and in complete control of my faculties.

I have a stack of *National Geographic* magazines sitting on my kitchen table. Why is that? In theory, this is my favorite magazine, filled with integrity and the beauty of nature, never polluted with cheap advertising, makeup, sex toys, all manner of gimmicks unneeded.

Never is there an article about the latest use of lasers, without some damn good reason like the betterment of humankind; nor the removal of crow's-feet. They never resort to computer-generated photos of how Gwyneth Paltrow might look with a bigger nose or hairless body. No tawdry stories delving into the unsolved suicide of some lost or lonely heiress, no exposés of insider trading, no rise and fall of a rock model superstar, no scandals or hopelessness, no tales of religious zealots castigating the liberal left. No, not even teenage lovers' sick pacts to murder their rivals. None of that—only wonderful journeys into still-exotic lands, inspiring photography capturing gorgeous little Chinese children, mountain ranges filled with majesty, carnivores and brilliant spiders, the Earth from a spaceship, hoedowns and barbecues, Texas cowboys, Brahmans, rare gems and dinosaur eggs, sperm whales and geishas, mummies and sunken treasure.

It's all there, without leaving home. You can share the travels of a lifetime, and yet—why is it?—my stack of *National Geographic*s is sitting there, pages still fresh with static, unread, untouched. There they sit, dating from 1995, all the months rushing by. All the crap I've read and tossed out, and still my magnificent *Geographics* sit with dignity on my kitchen table each day. I swear I'll get through them. Give me strength and guide me, please.

Bruce Springsteen—another song about a coal mine and the girl he had to leave behind.

I just got word that Nikko died in London. She was the second German shepherd puppy I bought for Sally after Marilyn got hit by a car in front of our house ten years ago. She was a sensitive girl, right from the start, shy, nervous, self-conscious, sweet, and protective; she always knew when I was down, and she would crawl up onto the bed and lie alongside me, nuzzling and licking my face. When Sally was mean, she always took my side. When Sally moved out of the house in 1988, I had to disconnect from Nikko. It was painful and sad, but I saw her once in a while up in Laurel Canyon, where they had moved.

One day I was standing out in the front yard and a woman pulled up to the house; a dog jumped around in the backseat. "Christ, that looks just like Nikko!" and of course it was. Sally had gone out of town and left her way up in Laurel Canyon, when this woman caught her and threw her into the car. She was still wearing tags from Blix Street: Sally hadn't bothered to change them. Nikko ran to me and flipped over on her back. I scratched her tummy and brought her inside. I knew I should have kept her right then and there, but like an idiot I gave her back to Sally when she returned home. Next thing I knew, Sally had given her to some English actress in Malibu named Elizabeth. "Oh, great, just what

Nikko needs—to endure the trauma of a new owner."
Then I figured maybe it was for the best; she'd get more
attention.

A few months later the actress moved back to London
and Nikko was in quarantine for six months, eventually
taking up residence in London. Quite some time went by
before I heard any more about her, until Cindy and I were
catching up and Nikko came up. "Well, yeah, I guess she's
fine living with Elizabeth Hurley and Hugh Grant." "Wait
a minute, that's the Elizabeth that took Nikko?" "Yeah—
she's the German shepherd in all the pictures with Hugh
Grant after the whole Divine Brown scandal; he's out in
front of their house walking her." "Jesus, wouldn't you
know it. Only Sally would manage to get even our dog into
a superstar family."

Famous or not, I knew Nikko and I can still remember
her lunging at the car window at an Armenian Texaco gas
attendant. She freaked at certain men. No, Nikko should
never have been moved around like that. She died of cancer,
poor baby. You know, it's weird how emotions can get so
entangled with an animal. You can think of their teeth or
the way they slept, jumping in their sleep, dreaming of big
fields and juicy steaks.

I haven't had a dog since Nikko. I'm starting to think
I'm shut down or scared, but more and more I long for that
friendship and love. You can think of those little things and
it brings out all the great and terrible things you had with
that person, and yet somehow it's dogs that make you cry
the hardest. You can't tell them you're sorry or that you
never meant to let them go. You can see their shining eyes,

smell their hot breath, feel them following you up and down the hallway, listen to you talk on the phone, wonder what world you're dreaming in. They know it all, but somehow you just can't ever make them know enough of how much you love them.

Lyrics for a New Musical

There has been many a plague in Great Britain
And yet I have never been bitten.
There's been maybes,
There's been scabies,
but never a case of rabies.
I've been smitten
but never, never bitten.
I'll confess here in Leicester
but I would rather not fester,
because there's never been a case of rabies in Great
    Britain before!

A Minor Traveling Alone
A script I'm writing for Lacey Chabert.

A Conversation with a Teacher of Disabled Adults

What do you do for a living, in three words or less?
—I teach art to disabled adults, mentally disabled adults.

Draw! Draw! Draw, you fucking moron! I don't want any more fucking excuses from you, OK?

Here! Take your pills and draw me a pretty little picture!

Get this guy on the potter's wheel—that'll be good for some laughs!

Oh, you know I love being in this town; I love being in this business. But there are some nights and some times, wouldn't it just be easier to throw in the towel and meet some nice guy, just betray all my real feelings and beliefs, move to some small town, raise a family, and just let it go, wouldn't it be beautiful? There are some dreams that die hard, ladies and gentlemen, and tonight I don't want to feel that I've ever betrayed myself or you; but there are times when I swear I just want to leave and run out and be there for somebody else.

If I Married a Doctor . . .

Look, honey, let me buy you a new car. What do you want—a Mercedes, a Lexus? You name it."

"No, I don't need a new car, sweetheart, my '91 Acura is just fine."

"Listen, my wife can't be seen running around in an old Acura."

"Your wife? What about me as a public figure? I've been running around in it just fine. So far, no one has thought the worse of me."

"Well, that may be true, but when you swing by the hospital to pick me up, you're my wife, and people will notice you for that, and they'll think I'm some kind of cheapskate, as if I married you because you were set up already and you're there to make me look good."

"Honey, look, I understand; but I think it's going to be OK, even if the other doctors see me in the Acura. Let's sleep on it, baby."

Last night my bed became a Native American sweat lodge.

A Dream

I'm in a bedroom. Lexie, Lil's friend, is in bed. Nicky comes in to hang out with us. Lexie wants to make love and so do I, but I don't want to hurt Nicky, so I stand in the room feeling melancholy. "It just hit me today, this is my last day of high school; can you believe it?" "Wow!" the girls exclaim, "that's amazing!" Finally we get the message across to Nicky that we want to be alone, in a nice way, and she leaves. We all kind of laugh. Lexie is being a little cold, but I know she's scared that her mom may come back. Since her brother's been kidnapped, her mom is very overprotective, even though she has an important job working on the underwater rescue team, so we know our time together is tenuous. She helps me undress. Two of the buttons on my flannel shirt are caught around shredding threads; we laugh uncomfortably. I'm flooded with conflicting emotions—I'm old, I'm young, where am I? Why do I still desire such a young girl? But I'm so young myself, I crawl under the sheets and lie in her arms discovering that these are the twin beds from my childhood and they are now too short for me. It makes me smile. We are kissing (I've tried to lock the two doors in the room—one leading into the hallway, one into the bathroom—but they keep popping open), we are passionate, and we feel so close—suddenly people burst in. I think someone says, "It's Patty" or maybe it's Lexie's mom. It turns out to be Fran, looking young and beautiful, the way she looked when I met her. I'm so glad to see her. I get up and hug her, introduce her to Lexie and Nicky. She's holding all these photos that she hands to me. We start looking at them: weird pictures of mentally retarded black people in the thirties, with big teeth and flat foreheads; some grotesque as if they were in concentration camps—emaciated, skin and bones, with big pigtails sticking out. Some of the pictures move like an old projector, battle scenes of these people dressed like African warriors carrying spears, while soldiers shoot at them. I can't look at them anymore. Lexie and I walk with Fran; the ocean is gray and misty. Fran takes my hand. "You must have married democracy," she tells me proudly; "just look at all these good girls around you." I look at Lexie with so much love. "Fran was my first love." We are all so connected, and it feels so safe.

Another Dream

I'm lighting candles on all these little cakes for you; it's your birthday. Carefully, I'm trying to carry them into the other room to set on a table so that you can blow them out; but every time I take even a step, all the flames go out. I keep relighting them and relighting them. The frosting is melting; the candles are dripping wax all over the place. Eventually, I feel so desperate I even use matches as candles; they sit on the cake charred and burned out. Two Hispanic men walk into a room where I'm sitting. One has a deformed face like the elephant man. I'm afraid of him, but I know I have to get over the fear and touch him, so I move over and sit next to him. He shows me a photo of how much his face has changed, and I'm caressing his cheek, telling him it's going to be OK, that it's part of his *tikune* and that he's beautiful already. He has a plastic cap on his skull. I feel such love and compassion for him, just letting him know that everyone suffers in their own way, but for him the light that is revealed will be greater.

You're channeling down everything from the universe. You can feel Mars. You can feel the floods on Mars, floods you've never seen here on Earth. I wake up with that vision, and it's a big responsibility, you know, to see things so far out from another world. And then you're not sure how you really feel, how you really feel, how you really feel, how you really feel. But you've got to walk tall and be strong, because we are of this Earth and sometimes it's a sad reminder of how many lifetimes we've tried to work through these feelings, these emotions, these notions. I see the oceans on Mars, and you know I wake up at night and I want to scream because I'm all alone, I'm all alone. Even now, when you're lying next to me, I'm all alone. I don't sleep with the TV on anymore. I used to sleep with the stereo blaring in the night. I would wake up, hear Cat Stevens, and it would make me cry. I didn't know why I was crying and I didn't know why I wanted to lie back down again. And I don't even want to say the word now, because sometimes you know you have to walk tall and be strong, even if you're all alone. Walk tall and be strong.

When I lie in bed at night I think about my dad and the last time I spoke to him, on his seventieth birthday. He would barely hug me and barely look me in the eye. I said, "Hey, why, Dad, why? Because I'm not under your thumb anymore?" You know, it made me sad, but my mom's always there, and I count my blessings for that. Sometimes the unconditional love of my mom is the only thing that pulls me through. I'm not a child anymore, can't you see? I'm not a child anymore. I'm a woman, and that's a big responsibility. I wake up at night, and I swear that I see the rivers on Mars, and the full moon. It shines down and it makes me new, and I start to wonder if I will ever have a baby of my own. Will I ever make my home a place where it won't be so lonely, where it won't just be me only?

Sometimes you've got to stop intellectualizing and asking all the questions, so I scan the *Zohar* and meditate on the Hebrew letters. It gets me through. And I have you and you and you. I don't mean it in a Diana Ross sort of way as much as I try to reach out. And G-d knows I've reached out and I've touched all the little people and the lonely people, and the people who aren't sure, and the people who are sexually ambiguous, and the people who think I'm so absolutely grounded. Then why do I have to adjust my own mike stand? Tonight I did my own hair, or I didn't do my own hair because I said be real, it's summertime, feel what you feel. And I swear, sometimes I wake up at night and see the rivers rushing down all over Mars. And I applied my makeup tonight after I cried all afternoon in my very pretty bedroom. The light filtered in just right. I just got my house painted, so it felt fresh and it felt new. I could still smell the smell of paint, and it really opened up my heart. Can you relate to that feeling of cleanliness and perfection?

I look through my closet, and everything is jammed into it. I have so many clothes and so many things that people have given to me. I'm a lucky, lucky, lucky girl, and I would never want to rub your noses in that fact. And my skin is soft; I take really good care of my skin because I love the skin I'm in, so I rub the lotions in. I applied my makeup very carefully for you tonight, not too much, not too light. I felt vulnerable; I did not know what I was going to say. Sometimes you don't know what you're going to say; sometimes when you're walking down that alleyway, sometimes someone wants to turn you on to something really bad. Sometimes it makes you really angry, and sometimes it makes you sad; but tonight I want to shed my skin. I love the skin I'm in, I love the skin I'm in and I want to win. I want to win and I want to let you in. I don't want to be bad, and I don't want to be sad, and I don't want to feel that I'm not fulfilled. I want to summon down all the spirits tonight, all the good spirits in the universe because I feel Patti Smith and I feel Laura Nyro and I feel Joni Mitchell and I feel all the good people tonight. Why did Laura Nyro have to die? Why did Laura Nyro have to die just to have her music played when there's all this mediocrity clogging up the airwaves? I remember the day—sitting in my mom's car in Phoenix, Arizona—that my favorite station went from AM to FM. I remember that day as if it were yesterday. I would sit in my bedroom with the blue-green shag carpet, and the astrological wallpaper, and I was playing Joni Mitchell's *Ladies of the Canyon*. I was imagining my future; I was imagining the night in my bell-bottoms, and my Indian beaded belt, and my skinny little body, and my first stereo. My dad walked in and turned it off in the middle of the night. "Hey, Dad, leave my stereo on because I'm all alone out here in the desert. I'm all alone and I'm scared because I don't know where I come from. Did I really come from you? Are you really my dad, or did I just show up from the moon? Because I swear, sometimes I wake up at night and I can see the mountains on Mars. I don't know who I am and I don't know where I've been, but I'm so glad I'm in the skin I'm in tonight. Sometimes I don't know what I want to say and it takes me this way. You lose love and you win love, and sometimes it just passes away. You cry for the people you've lost, and you try to figure out a way to get them back, but there's no way to get them back. So you let it go and you summon down from the universe all the sacred stars and light. Tonight I think I'll be all right. I guess I'll be all right tonight because sometimes you've just got to hold up your head, walk tall, be strong, and put on a little bit of an act. That's where I'm at.

Someone reached out to touch you in the summer darkness. There is a sound outside the window, but you can't move. The wind blows, and you suddenly recall who you were a thousand years ago. Love holds you here, as it always has held you. You're a child and a woman and a dreamer and you recognize all the signs of life, but you can't move.

It's time to go home to L.A.

She calls to me with her tainted air and majestic mountains, with oceans kissing the worn beaches, foggy Junes, barbecued Julys.

How this city has changed! There used to be hookers up and down this strip dressed to the nines, right across the street where I use to perform sometimes. I would go on at one in the morning in front of ten people. Paul Mooney was my mentor, and we used to scare everyone. Me in big funky high heels, Paul in cowboy boots. After one night of dancing, I observed, "I know why there's no Jewish hookers," and Mooney replied, "Now I know why there's no nigger cowboys." We would eat at Ben Franks. All the pimps in those wide-brim hats would nod to us and pay their dues to those funny motherfuckers.

There is only one House of Pies left in L.A. along with Farrell's ice cream parlors and other great West Coast landmarks of the seventies, swept away by more art-directed contrivances. We wonder whether or not it is a good thing to long for a good, flaky cherry pie under fluorescent lighting or giant bowls of ice cream with plastic zoo animals sprinkled over the whipped cream and nuts; to feel the sentimental tug at your heart for moments that needed no MTV stories or write-ups in *Vanity Fair*.

Southern California has been so overdeveloped that they might as well just build the entire coastline into one huge strip mall. At this point, we should just be able to walk from one strip mall to the other without interruption. There's no point to space—why should we have empty space? We don't want it. Empty space just scares us. They even have to build up the desert because there is just too much beautiful, star-filled land. Why have the terror of walking out into the desert night with emptiness and silence? You might have to question your reason for living. No, no—the simple solution is another strip mall! I'd rather buy some bulk groceries at a discount than walk around the desert. Long live strip malls!

She limped out of the grocery store with a screwed-up face. I mean, she was crying, hunched over, rubbing her ankle, and there was some kind of glistening, gelatinous sticky stuff all over her side and right hip. You see, she had been running up and down the aisles with her cart at full speed, so mad, freaked out, hair flying, that she lost control next to the imported jams, the ones with the picnic table-cloth tops from France. People stopped to help her, but, humiliated, she started swinging her arms and shaking her fists at everyone passing by. An employee refilling canned goods tried to calm her down, and she pelted him with cans of cling peaches. What a sight—her running out through the electric doors, screaming, cursing, talking to her sister, who wasn't on the premises at the time. She spit at me too, which scared me. I started thinking maybe she had TB, so I ran into the store right to the "personal" aisle, where I broke a seal on a bottle of Sea Breeze and poured some into my hands. No one noticed, and since I didn't really want the whole bottle I set it back on the shelf and started my shopping.

One Chinese Lantern: A New Broadway Musical

One Chinese Lantern, foreshadowing all the Chinese lanterns that could be.

If I could only sit down tonight I might feel a little bit different about everything; if I could only rest my weary legs and hurry home to my empty bed; if I could only clear my sadness from . . . "Charlie! Thank you, honey." That's Charlie and he's my friend; he's always here for me, even when I denigrate the Chinese, if you please. If I only had a stool tonight that I could carefully pull behind me so as not to make people think I'm too strong when I'm trying to be vulnerable, because G-d knows I could pick up this chair and heave it across the room. Let me move this so you can see me too—peekaboo. They spare no expense here at Luna Park. Look at my music stand; it's falling apart. Perhaps if I move it around two or three times, it will tighten up. It doesn't seem to be getting any tighter, but that's the charm of Luna Park, the one Chinese lantern illuminating the dark that makes me feel that you and you and you and you will be here with me too. I went to see a fabulous play—I felt I could have written every line. As a matter of fact, I did, and they stole it from me sometime in the night because I always talk in my sleep. Somebody was staying with me that night, and they used that same theme, but I let them have it, because I'll dream again and again and again. I'll write another show, but that's as far as they'll ever go!

They don't write good musicals anymore, because anyone can write a musical: "He came into my room and he loved me and he stole from me and he hurt me and he fucked me over and I love him I love him I love him what can I do, I'm obsessed I need to go to Lovers' Anonymous or whatever the fuck they call it. Can't you see I'm in desperate need of help? Help me! I love him, I need him, I moved into a big giant apartment that I shared with lots of friends and I thought the fun would never end. I did drugs, I mainlined, I fucked up, I got a really weird disease. I don't care if my eye is yellow. Am I standing behind a purple sign? Certainly some sage will cure it all. Can I have some antibacterial soap; I'm a dope! OOOOO, baby, yeah, I said I can't stand up straight anymore since I became an eighty-five-year-old black woman. I am singing and singing and singing and singing the blues for all the years I was with you."

Welcome to the Vine Street Bar and Grill, ladies and gentlemen. Dr. Nina Simone will not be able to make it this evening because she's out collecting her *Porgy* money!

Thank you, ladies and gentlemen. I've been in this business for many, many years and I plan on continuing it tonight with you. You've given me the power to go on. Good night. I love you. I'm narcoleptic; I'm falling asleep at my own tired shit!

Behind Your Back in Front of Your Face
A new film I'm writing for Gena Rowlands.

Tears Are by Special Order Only

My sister doesn't see them from her side of the room. Mom never worried while baking a casserole. Distant family members cajole, but rarely inquire. If these are the years of wonder, I did my best to play them down.

Ready or not, here I come. Quiet, sexy, very tall. Getting to know myself. Late nights sketching mountains and ponies. Watching my bones grow, my breasts swell, my blood flow. Mom dresses me up for proms and cotillions. I drive boys wild if I want to, but I don't—I'd rather talk; so would they. Matt is holding me close; he's the prize every girl wants to win. If there's a tragedy waiting to happen—double-page memorial in the yearbook, etched around the border in black, with one-line remembrances of our beautiful blond boy hero—it will be him. I sense it like a Gypsy, so I savor the romance of fate. Christian boys really know how to hold back. On the golf course we walk in the dark, stopping to take off my high heels and wrapping my arm around his waist; the salt, English Leather, the shedding skin of boyhood stick to my tongue.

Oh, Jesus, I love him. Knowing it is not meant to be, I show him my tears, sick, sappy, bubblegummy. The feel of his naked ass in my hands liberates me. Well, I think I left just about everything behind on the seventh hole—petals of carnations, a pearl earring, cinnamon panty hose. I was waiting for the years to go by just to remember this night. We all love to stab ourselves with knife-sharp rec-ollection, don't we? That's where I'm at right now. Trying to focus, but always slipping back into the tender drama.

My sister tells me, "Trust, sugar, is something I've always carried around with me like a condom in a guy's wallet. Every day I look inside to see if it's been damaged, if the package is still intact, if the liquid hasn't all oozed out. You see, it is a fragile thing, and I don't want to risk a disease of my heart if I should go and love someone dangerously. Once you've crossed that line, you won't ever be the same again. I can't afford that possibility. I know for sure, because it seems G-d only allows one or two fuckups before you simply can't regain your footing ever again."

I love my sister more than anything in the world. In better times we tore up many a town, stripping and drink-ing, generally wreaking havoc on so many poor guys. Lida is a real gorgeous lady, tall and slender, with hot red hair—a walking contradiction of carefree, toss it to the wind, I-don't-give-a-shit backdrop, to soft talking in whispers—wiping her eyes on some young boy's shirt when everyone feels it's over, deep potent melancholy. She is generous to the bone, trust me, because when I was failing miserably at just about everything life has to offer, she gave me hair-dressing school when I begged for it, real estate when I promised even myself to try to elevate our lives, right down to a screwed-up quickie divorce to a man she spotted as a prick-driven ego. Oh, no, Lida never let me down, and she barely lectured me for all the stupid selfish shit I pulled. I love her so much.

I remember the day we left home—our parents chasing us five blocks, complete with spit flying; my daddy's face red like a tomato ready to split and splatter; Mama, weeping like something out of a John Steinbeck dust bowl epic. It was a sight. After wrecking Daddy's Buick, and boys slipping in and out of our bedroom, we brought total chaos and shame to our family name. Lida never looked back: "Sugar, you are the love of my life; little sister, sweet honey thing, we will come home someday with big success and riches. This will all be forgotten; they'll all laugh and hug us; we'll shine like the stars we are."

This is just a sliver of the story I'd like to be able to tell you. I hope and pray that I do it the justice it so deserves. When I told Lida I was going to write it all down, our life up to now, she sat up in the bed. It was so late and the sky was moonless and lonely, but I could see her beautiful smile in what little light came through the window. "You do that, sugar; you've always had such a tender way with words. Tell it all: that time we saw a black man swinging from a tree holding his baby girl. The smells of all those towns we passed through—the families staring with big Keene painting eyes. How about the guy who fell in love with you so bad you sent him to night school, stuck by him when you knew you couldn't really love him all the way? We had to just up and leave Memphis in a heartbeat. Never saw a man cry like that, poor thing, and you were ready to kill yourself with guilt. Honey, you've *been* there! I don't want to think of life as so sad, hurtful, but you can't even turn on the damn TV, with a hundred thirty stations pumping out all that dark poison; seems like the devil has taken on a whole new business. You've got to write about the good times, sister, or I swear I'll lose my mind!"

I stayed up all night, sitting on the porch, listening to the night sounds, wondering if we would ever settle in somewhere, brushing away any number of flies. Lida slept. I listened for her breathing, for any crazy thing she might say in her dreams; I waited for the light of early morning to creep through before I lay down myself. Everything was stirring when I shut the door behind me. I sat on Lida's bed, kissed her warm head. My big sister—she kept us moving, forever linking up; gently she would bring my head back around when I looked too long behind us. She wasn't one for regrets: "Sugar, I can't undo the wrongs or injustices, but I will let everyone know I welcome this new day with great hope, complete confidence. I'd love nothing more than for you to join me." You can see that kind of beauty in her face, especially while she's sleeping; so as she was waking I let myself relax for a while, trusting that my sister would begin the new day in the right way for us both.

Angle on a woman walking alone down a street in the early morning. Some trucks pass by; a coffee shop fades; a gas station. She wraps her coat tightly around herself, adjusting a smart bag.

Voice-over:

"I'm not a hooker; let's get that straight right up front. I'm not lost or a victim. Do I drink? Like a fish. Stumble out of bars or beds, or strangers who scare me in the morning light? No. Did my father abuse me? Not that I can remember. Am I tough as nails packing heat; can I circumcise you with the mere look in my eyes, am I jaded, fed up with *men*, a competitive bitch to other women, mistrustful, bitter, aloof, and cold? Sorry, that isn't me in a nutshell. Maybe I'm a drama queen, someone who comes into your life just to fuck it up, make it chaos—a screaming banshee in the middle of the night, creating overdose scenes that end in emergency rooms, begging forgiveness and performing agitated sex acts with bandaged wrists. Stop! Don't take me to that place!"

I could be a perky secretary in San Francisco meeting you at Fisherman's Wharf for a crab Louie. Dancing languorously in the night to Burt Bacharach. A stewardess on Sabena Airlines sporting a perfect manicure.

I was completely devastated when John Kennedy finally got married. Like every girl in the world, I had some part of me that held out this fucked-up fantasy that I would be the woman that Jackie approved of on her deathbed. I know it's deep, but life could be that wacky, that insane, that Jackie's last whispered words would be, "Marry Sandra Bernhard." And then she drifted off as John-John began panicking.

When Jackie was redecorating the White House, citizens were donating money right and left. When my cousin sent in her contribution, she received a handwritten thank-you note from Jackie. So of course I wanted a handwritten letter from Jackie Kennedy. I sent in my five dollars. And I never got my handwritten thank-you from the First Lady. So I sent a letter saying that I had mailed in a contribution, but had never received a letter from Mrs. Kennedy. Soon thereafter, I received not only a letter of apology from the White House but a genuine, handwritten thank-you from Jacqueline Kennedy—which I lost, along with a letter of apology from Jerry Lewis for making fun of my lips on the set of *The King of Comedy*. Two of the coolest things in the entire universe, and I lost them. I think this is maybe the only thing that I regret in my life.

Gina Gershon is my new Dykon. Not to be confused with daikon. She's not a spicy salad mix, although she is mighty spicy. I loved her in *Bound*, not to mention *Showgirls*. In one she played a butch dyke and the other she played a sort of dyke. I love her diversity.

This "lesbian chic" thing has got to stop. Not that I don't love every minute of this "dyke awakening," but people are bound to get hurt. Or should that be spelled "hert"? Just because a straight woman suddenly decides to start making out with another woman and telling her how in love she is does not mean that she's a lesbian. It's like those college girls who are LUGs—lesbians until graduation. Oh, sure, you can fall for their act. But, honey, even when they're eating your pussy, they're still straight. Fags are going to be reading this in total bewilderment. It's not the same with them. Trust me. Once your husband starts taking it up the ass, you can basically rest assured that he's gay. There's no such thing as FUGs—fags until graduation. Oh, wait, yes, there is. Except they call them DFBs—Drunk Fraternity Brothers.

You know, Barbra Streisand won't let you photograph the right side of her face, only her left side. What does she do in real life? Keep her head constantly turned to the side, shrouded in shadows and mystery? How much different can the right side of her face be? If we finally see it, are we just going to scream? Is it that horrible? Front on, it looks fine. Suddenly from the side it's a deformed nightmare? I don't buy it.

Kris Kristofferson must have been nipping at the bottle during *A Star Is Born* to fake the hots for Barbra. Don't get me wrong, Barbra was a babe when she had the long hair, the pageboy, and could toss the shit around and balance out the face. I know, I need it too; I've got strong features. You won't see me in an Afro anytime soon. Not in 1998, 1999, or the new millennium. Not only that, but the hot pants with the *tuchis* hanging out. What was that moment? With Ryan O'Neal? Honey, she will work the sex angle.

All my life, I worshiped Barbra. I met her one time at the Academy Players screening of something. She was wearing a big hat (probably to keep me from seeing the right side of her face). I was standing three steps below her, thank G-d. If I had been taller, she probably would have pulled out a gun and shot me. I was totally nervous, but I worked up the balls to say, "Uh, hi, Barbra." Not a word. She just looked down at me from her perch. She froze me the fuck *out*! But I still love her.

Barry White for McDonald's

I was a vegetarian until I heard Barry's sexy ad.

Dreams

What I long for more than anything right now is consistency in my life, so I will create it and manifest
clarity
certainty
space
balance
beauty
strength
purity
joy
expression
creativity
love
health
friendship
warmth
coolness
water
fresh
flowing
endless
light
compassion

forgiveness
discipline
work
green
happiness

Where's my father?" he asked in a very determined voice. "He's dead, or rather he never existed." I blew out a big puff of smoke and looked him in the eye. "How could you do that to me? What am I, some bastard of the universe?" He was ready to hurt me, and I was frightened for a moment: "That's not the situation, and you know it. I don't think I ever misrepresented anything. I love you and that's why you're here." "Love, is that enough?" He crumpled into a heap on the floor. "Yes, love is enough and it's the only thing that matters."

Somebody's baby is crying; it seems no one can stop that pain. When I hear it, it sounds as though someone is dying with the whisper of lightning and rain.

If I could catch this falling star that rambles on so near the dark, there might be a better day that dawns with you, all words to pray.

Somebody's mother is walking; the streets are glistening, so damp; the journey is endless. Sorrowful temptress, lost in meditation, traveling on sedation, searching for roads on a map.

I am standing on the bank of a wild river in Idaho, twenty-three years ago—Fred, Missy, Dad, Mom waiting for me to jump in; flat rocks half drenched in ancient algae; the dry bit crunching under my painted little toes—Noxzema fumes wafting up my nose—wanting to leap in with great abandon. Everyone is floating now in a raft; I'm scared to shit knowing they won't come get me. "Lessons, lessons, Tee Tee [my childhood pet name]," Daddy yells over to me. "Little girl, you've got to hunker down and just go for it, got to learn to endure the cold *and* the wet. We're going to love you for it too!" Edging into the river, I bite the bullet for love, but in my head I'm thinking clearly that there must be something wrong with my family for making me do this, laughing at my expense. Will they be happy someday when I keep my distance? Any wonder why I might put up a frosty demeanor? By the time I reach the raft and pull myself in, there's a whole new game going on, so I just get a slap on the back of the head to shake up the brain stem, while blowing my nose in the water.

Today is my forty-third birthday (*blienera baruchashem*). If we are not constantly expanding our vessels to desire more of the light, then surely it will be taken away from us to once again waken that desire; so if we are constantly working to maintain that appreciation, we will hold on to it. What better thought to have in your heart and soul on your birthday, and on this really beautiful day too? With the bluest skies and wispy clouds, the sun pouring over in abundance, coolest breezes soothing and inspiring, so many beautiful calls from the gang, flowers and sweet wishes, encouragement and honesty, connection to the world with a sense of certainty and compassion. A new life, on its way (*blienera bizathasem*), continuity, tenderness, company, health, light, love, evolution. This is what my birthday means for me this year—the desire to appreciate and to infuse my work, friendships, family, and new baby with all the goodness and light from *hashem*, from nature and all that is blessed and nurtured from above. This is my birthday prayer and my prayer every day—that I stay connected with that strength, and that my family, friends, loves, and baby are protected and on the path to love and health always. And dear G-d, with all my heart and soul, I thank you for all the amazing people, experiences, and light you bless me with. And dear G-d, I promise to continue to give back to the world all that you bless me with. Thank you, G-d, for your certainty and light. Thank you, G-d; I love you. Amain.

Tammy Wynette's last thought:
   "Damn, there's a lot of good times out there."